A Touch of Jesus

To Jean from your Texas cousins —

Blessings!
Janet Burton
Phil. 1:9-11

A Touch of *Jesus*

Stories and
Studies of
Women in the
Life of Jesus

Janet F. Burton

Pleasant W*o*rd

A Division of WINEPRESS PUBLISHING

Pleasant Word (a division of WinePress Publishing, PO Box 428, Enumclaw, WA 98022) functions only as book publisher. As such, the ultimate design, content, editorial accuracy, and views expressed or implied in this work are those of the author.

Unless otherwise noted, all Scriptures are taken from the Holy Bible, New International Version, Copyright © 1973, 1978, 1984 by the International Bible Society. Used by permission of Zondervan Publishing House. The "NIV" and "New International Version" trademarks are registered in the United States Patent and Trademark Office by International Bible Society.

Scripture references marked KJV are taken from the King James Version of the Bible.

Scripture references marked NASB are taken from the New American Standard Bible, © 1960, 1963, 1968, 1971, 1972, 1973, 1975, 1977 by The Lockman Foundation. Used by permission.

ISBN 1-4141-0468-5
Library of Congress Catalog Card Number: 2005903527

Dedication

To my best friend and encourager,
Jack;

And to all the women friends
I have treasured,
and from whom I have learned so much,
beginning in childhood
and throughout life…to this day
and beyond it.

Table of Contents

Table of Contents

PART IV: WOMEN TOUCHED BY JESUS' DEATH AND RESURRECTION............. 233

Confessions of the Author (By Way of Introduction)

It's much like finishing a good novel. I come to the end of this manuscript and feel reluctant to close the story and let go of the heroes. *A Touch of Jesus* brings out that sweet sadness in me.

The women in these seventeen stories–twenty or more of them, plus their families and cohorts—have become intimate friends. In the years of research, intuitive thinking, and respectful imagining, each has come to speak to me in her own way. I finish the writing and move on with my life, feeling as though I leave good friends behind.

This pilgrimage produced some other unexpected benefits for me. In studying the women, I found the men also growing dearer. Especially the eleven Apostles—Andrew, Simon the Zealot, John and James—they are clearer now than before. And Peter! Wonderful Peter! I shall look him up in the heavens one day, for he gives us permission to be human and to fail.

But mostly, of course, Jesus! For each of these stories highlights another shining facet of the Jewel Who Is our Precious Lord. *The real point of the book is getting to know Jesus better.* It might be called a Gospel from a woman's view. I have grown in the writing. My prayer is that you will grow with me in the reading and resultant Bible searching it may provoke.

This book has been growing on me for many years. Probably twenty-five years ago, when Jack was called to a city church, requests began to come from women's classes and groups. "Will you bring a devotional at our meeting?" "Could you do the Bible study for our retreat?" Randomly I began walking with the women in the four Gospel accounts of Jesus and found each one to be fascinating, begging for deeper study. In time the folder of notes marked "Women" grew fat. (So almost did I, from the wonderful desserts served at these events, but that is quite outside the realm of this confession!) Several times over the years I sat down to write the book, but it was not ready to be written. Writers know that feeling. It has to do with the timing of God's Spirit in our lives. This year was God's time.

Let me take you along on the journey to discover and write about a woman in the life story of Jesus. The first thing we must do is Bible study—days of it! Some of these women, like Mary of Nazareth, come and go throughout the Gospels. Others—I think about the prophetess Anna, or the woman who gave her last mite at the treasury—have a bare mention, just a verse or maybe three. The first step is always to read everything written in the Bible about the one in focus. And take pages and pages of notes. We make a list of every event in the narrative to clarify her story. We study the cross references, footnotes, and parallel passages, using several translations.

That done, we begin to chase the details by research. The Bible dictionary becomes dog-eared as we search every article that remotely relates. Patiently we endure the tomes—the seminary texts and other books containing background. Especially helpful is the classic, *The Life and Times of Jesus the Messiah,* by Alfred Edersheim—a priceless book! Methodically we comb the exposition in several different commentaries. Every resource we have on the passages is carefully heard. And we keep taking notes.

By now, surprising and delightful details have been discovered. Important life-truths are rising out of the background facts. We begin to circle, highlight, and scribble in the margins of the outline. The tablet is getting respectably full. So we put it all down for a while and enjoy the process of prayerful, creative thinking. Intuition figures strongly here. *Why was she in that place at that time when Jesus' life touched hers? Who else might have been in her life and her world that day? What had she endured before the Touch of Jesus recorded in the Bible account? What happened after it? How was she like us? What can we learn from knowing her?* Sometimes we realize—*she has no name! We must give her a name!* Up from the pages of our Bible she comes—changing from two dimensions to three. Back in time we go, trying on her sandals, experiencing in some measure how life must have been for her.

Pouring over our list of events from the narrative we ask, "Which moment in the story shall we highlight? Where could we set the story to learn the most? To open widest the doors of common experience and discover truths that caused God to include her in the sacred Bible text so long ago?" There is always so much more to her life than the gospel-writers could tell. After a while we scribble a big star somewhere on the list. Maybe it comes before her encounter with Jesus—maybe within it—or maybe after it. Now we begin to outline a fiction vignette which sets the Bible passage into a larger life context. Every possibility of the fictional portion must square with the research done in our Bible study. These are Bible people and we must try not to range beyond the "fences" of how life actually was in that day, or the revealed facts of the story.

At some point we move from scribbling to keyboard, and let the story flow in the warm glow of the Spirit of God. It is all coming together now. He is blessing.

And when it is drafted and the exposition has been added in such a way as to draw the reader into the Word of God itself, we study it hard a while longer. It isn't Scripture—it is a kind of historical fiction—but it has to be right. Like a sculptor molding an image we work with it, subtracting the doubts, and adding the "Touch Points," for we want to feel *a Touch of Jesus* on our own hearts, too.

Then we save it, print it, and hand the drafted copy to a theologian (in my case, my wonderful pastor/husband, Jack) for scrutiny. That's how all seventeen chapters began. At this point in the process, the fun is over.

Confessions of the Author (By Way of Introduction)

You probably do not want to hear about the dozens more editings, the search for a publisher, the struggle for titles, the worryings and prayings and continual smoothings and refinings. That is the *real* work of a writer—what takes the book from a warm fuzzy home out into the bookshelves of your world.

A reader's valid question at the onset might be, "Is this a book on women's issues?" *Not really.* It has never been my passion to beat a drum for a cause. This is no defense of women's ordination, or mutual submission, or their kin. I believe in some form of those causes, and in those who actively further them in a spirit of kindness and truth. But in this book my desire has been much gentler: *to discover each individual woman and hear what her life story says to women—to me—today.* Oh, you will hear a drum beat here and there, but that is not the heart of the book. The issues that surface in *A Touch of Jesus* are those that seem to flow naturally from each encounter with the Lord. Actually, Jesus (in my view) did not turn his ministry into an overt defense of women. Rather, he treated each woman with deepest respect, valued her gifts, and met her need, setting for us an example "that we should follow in his steps."

A careful reader will now be free to enjoy this book on several levels. Let each story surprise and delight you, but watch in every paragraph for the historical crumbs that fall from careful research. Jot questions, objections, ideas. Some of those will be dealt with in the expositions that follow each fiction vignette. But—*mostly this*—listen with your heart. The women in this book have come back because they have deep and wonderful things to say to us. As you get to know them, *Jesus will touch your heart, also.* And a day when we feel *A Touch of Jesus* is always a very good day!

—Janet Burton

A Note about Group Study

A Touch of Jesus lends itself very well to a group study situation. Warm inspiration can grow as women hear the fiction stories and then delve into their Bibles for deeper understanding. Valuable sharing and insights come from discussion and note-taking together. Life-changing decisions and personal growth often result. *A Touch of Jesus Study Guide,* complete with interactive lesson plans for leaders, and worksheets which may be duplicated for each attender, is available from the author's web site: www.burtonministries.org. *Visit us there!*

Part 1

WOMEN IN JESUS' BIRTH STORIES

Chapter 1

Waiting...

Elisabeth, Mother of John the Baptist
(Luke 1:5–25 and 39–80)

Once more she glanced out the open doorway toward the lower road. The sun had set over the Judean hills and lamp lights glowed in several neighbors' windows. Zechariah was usually home by now. Mounting the stone steps, Elisabeth climbed to the roof for a better look. No, no sign of them yet. Perhaps something had come up and he was spending an extra night in Jerusalem. The brisk evening air sent her quickly back to her hearth. She stirred the coals, hoping to keep the stew warm a while longer in case he was on the way.

Elisabeth was used to waiting. Forty years of being a priest's wife had made the routines of temple weeks familiar. Always for the big feasts, and at other times when the Abijah division was called, Zechariah and the men of his family traveled the hill country road to Jerusalem to serve. On those weeks, Elisabeth busied herself with the garden, or the goats, or with weaving or sewing. There was always extra to do when Zechariah was away. Then on the tenth day he would return, weary of body, but renewed in spirit. And life would resume.

How many more years would his bad knee permit him to make the trip? A while longer, she hoped. Temple weeks were the joy of his year. Priests never retire, but one day the journey would be too much. Sticking a straw into the coals, she caught a spark and lighted their two oil lamps. Then, straightening the folded blanket on the raised hearth, she sat down on it, thinking quiet thoughts in the dim evening light.

Yes, she knew how to wait. She waited for the bread to rise. She waited for the rains to come on the garden. She waited for shearing time so she could weave garments for winter. And she waited for Zechariah. Once she had waited for a baby, but that wait was long in her past. Sometimes waiting fades like the evening, or drowns in secret tears. A wave of sadness came from somewhere deep inside and moved her toward a small, wooden treasure chest beneath the lamp stand. Elisabeth hadn't looked inside for several weeks, but for some wordless reason she needed to touch her memories again.

On top her mother's dowry coins shone in the lamplight. She pressed them to her lips. Under them was the Persian silk veil Zechariah had brought her from Jerusalem's market last year. What does an old priest's wife need with an embroidered silk veil? But she smiled at its loveliness. Working her fingers down further into the chest, she finally felt what she was looking for. Still brand new, but a little yellowed from the years, it was the tiny gown she had made for the baby who never came. Elisabeth buried her face in the soft fabric and remembered the months of hoping, the nights of despair, when Zechariah held her close and calmed her empty sobs. Why had God not answered their prayers? How could she bear to live without a child? In the end, they had each other, and that had to be enough. God does not always share his reasons with his own, however loved.

Absorbed in memory, she missed the soft steps of the donkey laboring to climb up the path to the house. Asa snorted with relief as Zechariah pulled off the leather bags and saddle. Elisabeth quickly shut the chest and started for the side door. Under the shelter, Zechariah was tethering Asa beside the manger for the night.

"Shalom, my love," she said, taking the bags from him. He smiled and his lips responded, but no sound came out. She reached up to kiss him. "Are you sick? Lose your voice?" she asked. His eyes told her something was wrong. Zechariah shook his head slowly. Her left hand cupped his chin as her right wrist tested his brow. "What's wrong, Zechariah?" He turned to go before her into the house.

Inside, he pulled her small body to him and held her close. Pressing her ear to his chest she felt him sob. Alarmed, Elisabeth looked up into his face and asked again more gently, "What's wrong, Zechariah? Talk to me."

Sadly he pointed to his mouth and shook his head. "Angel" he mouthed, pointing skyward. "Baby," and he put his hand over her womb.

"Whatever are you telling me?" she asked, a bit impatiently. "Here…" and she moved toward the wall shelf. Rummaging a little, she came up with a wax tablet and stylus. "Here…write me a note so I can understand what you are trying to say."

Zechariah moved closer to the lamp stand and began to write words. "Angel in temple. Baby boy–John."

Looking over his shoulder in the dim light, Elisabeth strained to see and comprehend. "You saw an angel?" He nodded, smiling, and shielded his eyes with his hand. "A bright angel? Really?" He nodded again, relieved that she was deciphering his signs. "Where were you?"

Zechariah wrote again, "Altar incense."

"Then you were chosen to burn the incense before the Lord?" His smile told her she was following. "Wonderful! And what about a baby? Who's going to have a baby?"

Again Zechariah put his hand over her womb and smiled, tears filling his eyes.

Elisabeth was afraid to ask the next question aloud. Fixing her eyes on his she thought she knew the answer, but another disappointment would be too much to bear. "Us?" she whispered.

"Us," he nodded back. And then she was lost in his safe embrace.

Questions began to flood her mind. "How will this happen when I am so old? How soon?" Pulling away she shook her head, trying to comprehend. "John? Why John? And why did God send an angel to tell you? And why can't you talk? Did you lose your voice in the surprise of it all?"

To all these questions Zechariah shrugged hopelessly. Too many questions for a man of no words. He took the tablet again and wrote, "A sign."

"A sign," she read. "For how long?"

"Till the birth."

"Oh no!" she wailed.

"Supper?" he wrote.

"Oh! Yes, of course." And she turned to tend the pot on the hearth. "Who can cook with angels making announcements?" she laughed, and served two bowls of stew with bread from the morning's baking. Zechariah poured the wine.

As always, Elisabeth waited for her husband to ask the evening blessing, but no words came. Looking into his face she said, "I guess it's all right for a woman to say the prayer?" And without waiting for an answer, she spoke the familiar words, "Blessed art Thou, Jehovah our God, King of the world, Who causes to come forth bread from the earth." And then they ate in silence.

Supper over and dishes done, Elisabeth broke the hush. "It's late, my love, and there is a chill. I'll spread the mats." Reaching to the hearth she began to unfold the sleep mats and blankets. Beside them the tiny baby gown lay where it had fallen. She stooped to put it back in the chest, but then—on impulse—tucked it into her blouse.

Zechariah closed the doors, removed his sandals and outer cloak, and lay his weary body down gladly. Elisabeth snuffed one lamp, but left the other burning. Then, covering her husband, she crawled under the blanket beside him. In the dim flicker of light she felt his arm go around her and stretched to kiss his neck. Only a friendly cricket broke the silence. Elisabeth waited quietly. In just moments Zechariah's breathing grew deep and steady. This would not be the night to make promises come true. She lay nestled against him, her mind whirling from thought to thought, trying to process too much too soon.

"I must believe that what God says, he will do," she told herself. Her hand went to the tiny gown tucked close to her breast. Another wait. But this one would be joyful.

Behind the Scene
A Study of Luke 1:5–25 and 39–80

How Did Luke Know?

Only Luke, among the gospel writers, tells us about Elisabeth and Zechariah, and the birth narrative of their son, John the Baptist. What might have been Luke's source, or sources, for this information? He states clearly (Luke 1:3) that he constructed the book from personal research based on eyewitness accounts. Interviews! From whom did he learn these unusual stories on the background of John's family?

Luke was not reared in Israel. He was a Greek physician who first enters the Gospel narrative in Acts 16:10. Researchers believe he may have been from the area around Troas in Asia Minor, or perhaps from Northern Macedonia. His first recorded trip to Israel came when he accompanied Paul back to Jerusalem (Acts 21:15). On that visit, you may recall, Paul was arrested on false charges by the Jews, who had a contract out on his life. Luke seems to have been with Paul when he was transferred to the prison at Caesarea and also at Rome, off and on, for perhaps four years. With whom could he have spoken about John the Baptist during that time? Consider these possible of sources of his record:

James, the half-brother of Jesus, was the active head of the church at Jerusalem during the time Paul and Luke were traveling on his missions to Asia Minor, Macedonia, and Greece (Acts 15:13). John the Baptist and Jesus' family were related through their mothers, so the stories of Elisabeth and Zechariah would have been told often within James' hearing.

Jewish friends of Paul, such as Silas, who had been in Israel during the ministry of John the Baptist, may have known the stories circulating about his unusual birth. Weeks of travel and long prison days afforded much time to reminisce.

Many priests—former friends of Zechariah—had come into the early church (Acts 6:7). The visit of the angel to Zechariah would have been well-known in those circles.

John the son of Zebedee, Peter, and several other of the original twelve Apostles, survived Jesus and came to know Paul and his mission team well (see Acts 15:2). Some of these had been disciples of John the Baptist before following Jesus (John 1:35–36 and 40) so may have heard him tell firsthand of his beginnings.

Mary, Jesus' mother, or some of her close friends, may also have lived to talk with Luke. Mary was probably less than twenty years old when Jesus was born, and only near fifty when he died. Paul's imprisonment in Caesarea was thought to have come about thirty years later. Mary may have survived to age eighty. More likely some of her friends—Mary Magdalene or Joanna—were somewhat younger and still living. From them, Luke could have heard the stories from a woman's point of view.

Luke's gospel shows a particular sensitivity to women. In addition to Elisabeth, he alone tells us about the wonderful prophetess, Anna (Luke 2:36). And, while Matthew tells of Joseph's visit from the angel, only Luke recounts the story of Mary's encounter with Gabriel (Luke 1:26), her visit to Elisabeth, and her wonderful song of joy that we call "The Magnificat" (Luke 1:46–55). Some people wonder if Luke's background as a physician caused him to approach women in a more understanding way. These wonderments are interesting to explore.

Touch Point

Luke gives us a very perceptive insight into how the inspiration of the Bible happened. Without question we accept that Luke's gospel was God-breathed. Renew that faith by reading Paul's words in 2 Timothy 3:15–17. Because it is inspired, Scripture has a supernatural way of touching us deeply at key points in our lives.

Luke was a scientist, a doctor, and a researcher. Luke 1:1–4 shows us his heart. How does the inspiration of God through the

Holy Spirit interact with scientific investigation here? In what ways might God allow the personality and background of the author to show through in the Scriptures?

Now, before plunging ahead, read carefully the entire story of Elisabeth in Scripture: Luke 1:5–25 and 39–80. Keep a pen handy as you study further. If Elisabeth's story and the Bible exposition that follows inspire you to research further on your own, this book will have succeeded in its mission!

Living with Unanswered Prayer: Luke 1:5–7

There is a goldmine of clues about Elisabeth in Luke 1:5–7. On her father's side, she was descended from the priestly family of Aaron. Her husband had been chosen for her from the community of priests. We learn a few verses later (Luke 1:36 and 39) that she was also a relative of Mary, whose father had descended through the royal line of David and the tribe of Judah (Luke 3:31). This relationship, then, may have been through Mary's mother. Nowhere is it said exactly how Elisabeth was kin to the younger Mary—whether aunt, cousin, or otherwise—but from the story we can see that the bond between them was close.

Wonderful words describe the character and life of Elisabeth. She was a godly woman ("upright"), a faithful believer ("observing all the Lord's commandments and regulations"), and highly regarded among her neighbors and relatives ("blamelessly"). But Elisabeth lived with the deep sorrow of an unanswered prayer. She had never been able to conceive a child—the highest purpose of a Jewish woman.

No doubt Elisabeth grew up expecting to marry and become a mother. She may have wanted several children. In the early years of her marriage she surely expected each month to discover that a pregnancy had begun. Can you see her playing with her friends' babies and caring for her nieces and nephews, believing that soon she would have a child of her own? Perhaps she wove soft fabric and made infant garments—only to give them away as gifts to her friends that were expecting.

When during her long years of waiting did the fear set in that she might never be able to bear a child? How long before she realized her window of fertility was closing? How many times did she apologize with tears to her patient husband? Might they have together offered sacrifices, hoping to clear any obstacles of unknown sin that had caused God to close her womb? What did her friends say to console her? The burden of secret grief must have been almost overwhelming.

God's silence is always difficult to understand. In all those years of childlessness, no angel was sent to explain. Surely she could have coped if God had shared with her the secret that in her maturity she would conceive. But Elisabeth and Zechariah were left to deal with their disappointment through struggle, tears, and renewed faith in the wisdom of God. She could have responded differently—and perhaps she did at some point along the way. Unanswered prayer can cause even good people to become discouraged and to doubt the kindness of God. It is fertile ground for jealousy, bitterness, pretense, and rage.

We know that, at some point, Elisabeth released the matter into God's hands and determined to live well the life she had been given. Through years she was seen by others close by her as faithful to the Lord—a woman to be admired and respected. Bitterness, pretense, and their kin do not produce that kind of character in a woman. Only walking in faith day by day, living by the revelation of the Holy Scriptures, builds that quality of life.

Touch Point

Elisabeth's was a good prayer. She was seemingly within the will of God for her life and in keeping with the scriptural commands to a godly woman. In the heart of God, her prayer had already been answered. But the answer was not within her sight or of her timing.

Can you identify with Elisabeth's experience of unanswered prayer? Have you had a time of waiting for God to answer—and felt the silence of God? Has your life taken an unexpected or unwanted turn because of a prayer not granted? How did you react to "unanswered" prayer when it happened to you? Did you have negative attitudes to admit and overcome? To what person or source could you turn to help you accept reality and move on to live your life well, in spite of your disappointment?

With hindsight, can you see the kindness of God in making you wait on him? Or is that still ahead for you? Have blessings or lessons come from the experience?

The Unexpected Change: Luke 1:8–25

Elisabeth and Zechariah had chosen a quiet life in the country, not in the usual priest's settlements nearer Jerusalem. Luke tells us it was a small country town (1:39–40) and suggests that friends and relatives lived nearby (1:58). All of the men of Zechariah's family were priests—that was the assigned role of the descendants of Aaron. So, on temple weeks some would travel together to serve at the temple. The 20,000 priests living in Judea and serving in Herod's temple were divided into twenty-four family groups. Each division served only one week out of each six months, but all the priests were called to duty for the three major feast weeks. Besides those five weeks each year, Zechariah and Elisabeth lived the simple life of villagers, surrounded by gentle hills in goat country. They had grown older and comfortable with that lifestyle.

So how did Elisabeth receive the news that, in her old age, her life would totally change? If a baby does *anything,* he changes every aspect of life. Elisabeth's life was about to turn upside down, and even in her great joy at the prospect, she must have struggled with the adjustments she and Zechariah would have to make. We sometimes have to ask if we really *want* God to answer our prayers when the answer may result in the chaos of a lifestyle lost.

Perhaps we find a clue in Luke 1:24. For five months Elisabeth remained in seclusion, indoors, nurturing her secret happiness. Pregnancy was a much more private affair in those times. No over-the-counter tests confirmed the reality of her pregnancy the day after conception. Quietly she prepared, stitching swaddling clothes and small gowns, for the birth of their first child. Zechariah, no doubt, fashioned a cradle or bed, and maybe small wooden toys—the things a boy would like. Elisabeth wove blankets—activities friends their age were busy doing for their grandchildren! And she ate carefully, for the baby she carried was to be a Nazarite, separated to God for his work. She would choose not to eat grapes or raisins or drink wine, vinegar, or grape juice for the duration of her time. Later she would select a midwife to assist in the birth.

And, I like to think that as she waited for John to come, she remembered the ancient prophecies. I see her sitting with Zechariah by the open window, reciting to him from the Scriptures, and realizing that, if their son was the forerunner of the Messiah (Luke 1:17), then the Messiah would also soon come! Possibly in their lifetime! Redemption was near! God was about to fulfill his Covenant promise to bring salvation to the world through the descendants of Abraham—remarkably, themselves! No wonder Elisabeth's anxieties were tempered with a deep, deep joy. Her time, and Israel's time, of waiting was almost over. Zechariah must have watched her growth in silent, wondrous joy.

Touch Point

Can you share a time when God answered a prayer and the result brought change—and perhaps chaos—into your life? Did the up-heaval cause you to wonder if your prayer had been within the will of God? Do you look for the will of God always—or *usually*—to produce calm and peaceful results?

How conscious is your awareness of the greater plan of God and your part in it? When a prayer seems unanswered, do you ever think that God may have something greater for you to do at some future time? Or that your need may have to be sublimated to the bigger picture?

Sharing the Joy: Luke 1:39–56

Have you noticed now often, when we have a special need, God sends just the right person into our lives? That was the case for both Elisabeth and Mary. Luke tells us they were kin (Luke 1:36), but he does not tell us in what way. Mary needed a mentor, an advisor, perhaps to help her know how to explain her story to her family and fiancé. Elisabeth needed someone who could understand that hers was not just an out-of-time pregnancy but a special act of God. Both needed assurance that what they had experienced was truly divine. The Holy Spirit of God gave them *both* that certainty through a baby's leap in the womb. Two mysteries confirmed by a third.

In Zechariah's safe house, Mary was able to talk freely. Through the wisdom of the silent, old priest and his godly wife, this unschooled girl learned much. Out of the secret, pent-up meditations of her heart burst forth joyful praises to her God and Savior. And as the older embraced the younger, Elisabeth said, "Blessed is she who has believed that what the Lord has said to her will be accomplished!" (Luke 1:45) Had you noticed the *power* of that blessing before? Believe that what God has said, he will do! It's a promise for times requiring unusual faith.

Touch Point

Have you had the experience of God's sending someone to you just when you had a great need? Or have you been that person, sent to encourage a friend in difficult circumstances? Perhaps the messenger came by phone, or by e-mail or written note—or perhaps in person. Is there someone for you to encourage today? Listen for the urging.

Notice again the promise in Luke 1:45: "Blessed is she who has believed that what the Lord has said to her will be accomplished!" It may be worth your taking a few minutes to memorize. When do you think God could use that promise to your good?

Promises Fulfilled and Promises to Come: Luke 1:57–80

It may have been a difficult birth. Old bones resist stretching, and old muscles cry out against strain. But in time the day came, and Elisabeth knew that all systems were "Go." In a few hours Elisabeth's joy outweighed her pain, and she saw with her eyes the baby she had wanted for perhaps forty years. The midwife wrapped her precious boy securely and laid him on her trembling breast. Women of the community gathered around to adore, saying all the things we say at such times, wondering privately how this unusual event could have happened. (Some may even have dared to ask!)

They named the baby exactly what he was: God's gracious gift, *Yohanan,* "John." And with that act of obedience God released Zechariah from his silence. The joyful new father broke forth into praise. At long last he could talk again! God's promised salvation was now in process. The Messiah was on the way. The Holy Covenant was being fulfilled. A life of freedom and holiness was on the horizon. True, they did not understand the suffering Messiah that Jesus would be, but they rejoiced in the light they had that beautiful day in the hill country of Judea.

What parent does not look into the tiny face of his newborn and hope great hopes, dream great dreams? But for Zechariah and Elisabeth, the hopes and dreams were based on the spoken promises of God. Picture the old priest at this point in his song, reaching down to take his infant son from his wife's arms and holding him up for all the gathered crowd to see. Looking into his wide-eyed face, the father spoke to him words much too big for a baby's ears. "You, my son, will be a prophet of God, a forerunner of the Messiah, an evangelist to lead people to repentance, a bringer of light and peace."

Then, kissing his baby on both cheeks, he placed him back in Elisabeth's lap with a tearful smile, and they began their new life as parents of an unusual and gifted child. John was raised in the hill country, learning to love the outdoors (Mark 1:6), and he also learned to live off the land. He was strong *of* spirit, and strong *in* the Spirit. A rugged young man with a rugged task to do. Did his parents live thirty more years to see him grown? To hear him preach? Almost certainly not. But he brought them joy, and they would have been proud of the sterling character that carried him to the end.

For Elisabeth, the waiting had been well worth it.

Chapter 2

Chosen

Mary of Nazareth
(Luke 1:26–56, Matthew 1:18–25)

The third day of travel was just breaking dawn when Mary rolled onto her knees and folded her blankets. She was glad they would be home before sunset. The thought of another night on the road was not inviting. Even the kindness of her uncle and her caravan companions, who helped her pitch her shelter and shared warm meals with her, did not ease the aching of her back.

Stuffing her belongings into the travel bag, she swung it resolutely onto Uncle Jeremiah's cart and took a few bites of cheese and bread to help her get started on the day. If her Uncle had known her secret he would, no doubt, have insisted she ride most of the way. But for now, the walking felt good. She had plenty of things to think about before the group reached Nazareth.

Joachim would not be a problem. He would believe her story—or he would try to. Their bond was deep, and he would know in his heart his eldest daughter had not betrayed the family. She would find a way to tell her father first, counting on him to calm her mother when she heard the news.

But how to tell Anne? Mary was certain her very practical mother would not believe the story of an angel. No baby in the history of the family had ever been conceived but by the usual way, and Anne would not easily accept that her daughter was an exception. She would probably blame Joseph—*poor man*—and he didn't even know yet. And she would blame Mary for blemishing the family name and ruining the wedding plans. And she might even blame Joachim for taking her part in it all. It was likely going to be a messy time, and only her father's intervention could hold the lid on that boiling pot. Too bad Gabriel hadn't made a stop in Anne's kitchen before disappearing, leaving Mary herself to break the news.

A deep sigh came from somewhere beyond consciousness. The goat cheese hadn't settled too well. Maybe she would ask Uncle Jeremiah if she could climb onto the cart and ride a while.

Lying back on the bundles of travel bags, Mary covered her face with her veil to shield her eyes from the morning sun. The creaking and swaying soon put her to sleep, and it was midday when she felt the cart halt. Jeremiah released the donkey to graze and water while the travelers found shade and munched what dried fish and bread they had left. Someone found a date cake in the bottom of a bag and shared it around.

After eating, Mary walked to the nearby creek to splash her face and drink deeply. Just two hours to go, and now she must deal with the thing she had been trying to forget for three months—telling Joseph. It was time to tell Joseph about the angel—and the baby in her womb. She tried to remember Elisabeth's good advice. How had she said it? "This baby is Jehovah's miracle, and he will help Joseph understand." Mary hoped so. *Desperately* she hoped so. Joseph was too kind a man to hurt, and she was beginning to love him so. And, if Joseph did not understand—the thought overwhelmed her—probably *nobody* would. If he were to reject her, she could be a divorcee and an outcast for the rest of her life. And if they didn't marry soon, people would forever wonder about the baby and hold it against them. Mary was beginning to think maybe it would be easier not to be chosen by God, after all. The hurdles ahead seemed more than she could manage.

The caravan was gathering again, and Mary rushed to catch up. "Hurry, Mary Sunshine," her uncle called. "Not far now. I know you are very tired. Nazareth is just over that next rise. We'll be home before supper!"

Mary smiled at her favorite uncle—so much like her father, but a few years older. "Thank you for letting me travel with you, Uncle. Father was anxious about my getting home safely, but your trip to Jerusalem came just at the right time. I hope I haven't been too much trouble."

"None at all, my dear. Glad to have your company." Jeremiah smiled at this lovely niece, who had grown up just around the corner from his family. "Tell me about your wedding plans. You will be a beautiful bride. Are you excited about marrying Joseph?"

His question caught her a little off guard. "Very excited," Mary answered with a giggle, "and a little frightened. I'm growing up very fast, and it's a lot to think about." She stopped short of sharing her deeper fears.

"Oh, you will do fine," he assured her. "I've known Joseph for years. He is a good and gentle man, and he will treat you well. And you are a fine young lady. Joseph has made a wise choice." Jeremiah nodded approvingly. "You will have a good life with him. He's a hard worker. We are looking forward to having him in the family."

Mary nodded and squeezed her uncle's arm and then fell behind the pace with her thoughts. *How will I ever tell Joseph,* she thought? And for the umpteenth time she began trying out starters. *"Joseph, an angel came to see me one day, and I need to tell you about it."* She shook her head. Too unbelievable. *"Joseph, God has given me a special job to do, and I am with child."* Still not right—too direct. But she did want to be honest with him. Surely God would give her some words.

Finally, *"Joseph, I hope you will listen and believe me. I have something pretty awesome to tell you. God has chosen us for a special job."* Yes, that might do. In a way, God had chosen Joseph, too. Then he could ask questions, and she could tell him slowly, as he was ready to hear it. And if he could not understand? That, too, would be in Jehovah's hands. But she *would* be very sad.

The song was playing in Mary's mind again. Such joyful words, and she would have loved to sing them out loud. But it made no sense to anyone else, so she hummed quietly under her breath. "My soul praises the Lord and my spirit rejoices in God my Savior, for he has been mindful of the humble estate of his servant. From now on all generations will call me blessed." The words of this song gave her hope.

Uncle Jeremiah caught her eye and pointed with his walking stick to the horizon. "Just over the hill now, Mary. We are almost home." Mary peered into the late afternoon sun for a first glimpse of her hometown. Smoke from cooking fires was drifting over the hill in the afternoon breezes. The farmlands and rock fences were familiar now. Mary knew who lived in just about every house along the road from the Nain turnoff to Nazareth. The summer field flowers had died while she was away, dried by the long, hot days. But soon the rains would come again, and the pastures and vineyards would green up. Nazareth was a beautiful place when the rains came.

Susanna's goats were out again, eating the neighbor's garden—what was left of it. Mary giggled at the thought of the conversation to come. Amos shouted a greeting as he and his dog lumbered by, pulling his cart of milk goats back from a profitable day in town. As they came to the first terrace and started down into the village, Mary's heart quickened. Joseph's shop was just down from here, in the next block. She hurried to catch up with her uncle.

"Uncle Jeremiah, I believe I will stop by Joseph's shop on my way home. Thank you so much for a safe and comfortable trip." She bowed quickly, and he responded with a smile and a nod.

"I'll drop your travel bag off at your father's and let him know we made it safely. Shalom, Mary."

"Shalom, Uncle. I love you."

Her feet moved faster as she started toward the shop. In the three months with Elisabeth she had filled her mind with dreams and plans for her new home and baby. How she hoped Joseph would share her excitement and want to be part of her dreams.

The shop door was open to the afternoon sunshine, and she could hear sounds of working inside. She would have dashed in but dared not, for fear he might be alone. Looking in she called, "Joseph? Joseph? I'm home!" And in a blink he was out the door and beside her. His clothes were damp with sweat, and sawdust stuck to his beard and eyebrows. But all she could see was his smile.

"So you are!" he laughed, and hugged her warmly. "How was your trip? And why did you leave in such a hurry? And stay so long? Come inside and tell me about it." Noticing her hesitation he was quick to add, "It's all right. Mama is in the next room. Come on in." And he stepped aside to let her go first.

"It was a wonderful trip. Elisabeth and Zechariah are such dears, and they helped me so much. But, Joseph my love, I have something very important to tell you." Catching the seriousness of her tone, he sat back on the workbench, met her eyes, and held her shoulders in his strong hands.

"So, tell me…," he said softly.

"Joseph, God has chosen us to do a special job for him. Both of us. And it will change our lives."

His tone matched hers now. "What job? How do you know this? What are you telling me?"

"Just the day before I left a very strange thing happened. Late that afternoon, while I was resting from bringing water from the well for Mother, an angel came to me in my room. I know it sounds crazy, but it happened, Joseph. Please believe me."

"Go on," he said guardedly, realizing how very young she was.

"And the angel told me that I—we—had been chosen by God to have his special baby—his Messiah." The words were coming very fast now. "And I asked him how this could happen, since we have not been together yet, but he said God's Spirit would come on me and make it happen." She stopped to search his face.

"Go on," he said again.

"So I was afraid, but I told the angel I—we—would do what God asked."

"But Mary, the wedding is still three months away," he said patiently. "We can't have a baby yet."

"The baby is already on the way, Joseph. God has done his miracle. I'm going to be a mother." She felt his hands fall from her shoulders. His head dropped, and he studied the floor.

Without looking up he asked quietly, "So you are pregnant?"

"Yes, my love, but with *God's* baby. I have not been unfaithful—I promise! I would never do that to you, Joseph. But I think we must marry quickly—maybe

43

this week—or else people will talk." But he wasn't listening now.

Shaking his head, Joseph got up from the bench and walked a few steps away, his back to her, his shoulders bent. The room was silent, and Mary could hear her heart pound.

"Do you believe me, Joseph?" she asked quietly.

"I need some time, Mary," he responded softly. "I need some time. Come, I'll walk you home."

Mary read his face as he turned toward her. Suddenly she felt very alone. Fighting back her tears, she answered, "No, Joseph. It's still light. You have work to do before night, and I can walk it alone. Will I see you soon?"

"Soon," he said, and she turned and hurried out the door.

Behind the Scene
A Study of Luke 1:26–56 and Matthew 1:18–25

Why Mary? Luke 1:26–38

For generations Jewish maidens in the ancestral line of King David had known that one day a virgin girl would be chosen by God from among them to bear the Messiah. How many generations? In the unfolding of God's revelation, certainly by Isaiah's time in the eighth century B.C. the expectation was becoming clear (see Isaiah 7:14 and 9:6–7). Much they did not comprehend, but the coming of a Savior Messiah through the line of David was reasonably well understood and believed.

Now it was time—God's fullness of time—and who would he choose? A girl of marriageable age, yes, but from an out-of-the-way village in the backlands of Israel? One from a poor family with no recent outstanding relatives in her line? Among the wonderful mysteries of God is the *how* and *why* of persons he chooses for special tasks. Why, of all the men in Ur, did he select Abraham, the son of Terah? Why, of all the babies born and murdered in the latter days of Egyptian slavery, did he single out Moses, the son of Amram, and his father's sister, Jochebed? Why, of all the royal princes carried off captive to Babylon, did God commission Daniel to be a prophet to generations of Persian kings? Why Joseph of all the brothers? Why Simon Peter? Why Saul of Tarsus?

Historical record confirms God's wisdom in each choice—and underlines our woefully human habit of judging by outward appearances. In each case, as is no surprise, God chose well. Mary is no exception. Probably just marriageable age...maybe sixteen or younger...she must have had within her special qualities that God knew would carry her through the ups and downs ahead. Mercifully, Mary could not see all that would be asked of her. Probably she had not lived long enough even to guess at it. But throughout the chaos of Jesus' short career she was there—a tenacious Jewish mama, bearing all things, believing all things, hoping all things, enduring all things. Even to the Cross, and—*glorious day!*—to Pentecost. (We will pick up her story again in Chapter 17).

So, when Gabriel dropped in unexpectedly one spring day, Mary listened fearfully but intently, and understood enough to know that she was being asked to bear, without the natural intercourse of life, an infant Messiah who would rescue the people of God. Reaching beyond fear she asked, "How will all this come about, since I am still a virgin?" And in one brief sentence Gabriel explained what has become one of the most complicated and disputed doctrines of the Christian church: the virgin birth. Isn't it a wonder that finite man today finds it comfortable to argue with angels?

"I am the Lord's servant. May it be to me as you have said," Mary answered, accepting the angel's brief explanation. And now it becomes clear why God chose Mary. Stop and read the entire amazing scripture for this story before you pursue its truths in the study ahead.

GOD'S CHOICE

God needed a woman tender and mild,
to bear unto him his Holy Child.
A woman to nurse, to bathe, to swaddle,
and hold him to heart with loving cuddle.
God needed a woman tender and mild,
And found her in Naz'reth town.

God needed a woman patient and wise,
to teach his Son with each morning rise,
the words and stories from holy scrolls,
praise songs and prayers from sacred rolls.
God needed a woman patient and wise,
and found her in Naz'reth town.

God needed a woman with heart undefiled,
to show by her life to his Only Child
love for the people passing near by—
people for whom he would one day die.
God needed a woman with heart undefiled,
and found her in Naz'reth town.

Today God still seeks the tender and mild,
women with hearts that are kept undefiled;
those who will face each new sunrise,
determined to be both patient and wise.
God needs women like this today.
And he's searching in our town.

—Janet Burton

The Calm before the Storm: Luke 1:39–45

We bless Elisabeth. Someone had to be there for Mary, to counsel and mentor her. Anne and Joachim were a little too close to the situation. In small town Nazareth, neighbors would talk. But Elisabeth was a perfect support for her cousin. A three or four days' journey south, she herself was already part of the amazing plan—a little miracle on the edge of the most wonderful act God had ever worked in his world. God himself was coming to earth to live among men! Six months into her own unexpected pregnancy, Elisabeth believed. And there, in the home of Zechariah and Elisabeth, Mary found the refuge she needed to sort out her thoughts. There her joy could spill out and the incredible promises she'd received from God could be spoken aloud.

No wonder she stayed three months! It must have been hard to go home.

Touch Point

Do you have a place of refuge where you can go to be heard and held and loved and understood? Of course, to Jesus. And, if you are married, perhaps to a loving husband. But we speak here of a place outside yourself. A Thomas Kincaid painting is captioned, "I walked into the heart of a friend and found a home." Everyone, but especially women it seems, needs a place of full release. A place of spiritual guidance. Pray that God will give you such a place and such a friend.

Perhaps he will allow *you* to be that trusted someone in the life of another. The friend with an open heart and home. Life is so much easier to bear when someone shares the load with us.

The Magnificent Song She Couldn't Sing: Luke 1:46–56

Who but Elisabeth and Zechariah could listen to Mary's song and not judge her? "Thank you, thank you, for choosing me!" she seems to say in verses 46–49. She didn't ask *why* God chose her. In teenage wisdom she just laid it all out. "God does good things when he chooses to, and on whom he chooses to, without regard for status and power" (verses 50–53, author's paraphrase).

"And, always, he keeps his promises!" (verses 54–55). Words so insightful must have come from beyond her, and that, too, is explained. The Holy Spirit of God had overshadowed her, and now she was not the same simple peasant girl her friends and family had known.

Apply that backwards to Abraham, Moses, Daniel, and the other "chosen" ones mentioned earlier. Perhaps it was not so significant who they were when they were chosen, but who they became when God's Spirit indwelt them. A man (or woman) possessed of God is not a usual man—not a finished man. He is just a suggestion of who he will become. "'Not by might nor by power, but by my Spirit,' says the Lord Almighty" (Zechariah 4:6).

Touch Point

Have you wished to become more useful to God? To be chosen by him for something that will make a difference in the world? Try Mary's prayer on for size. Can you say with her, "I am the Lord's servant. May it be to me as you have said"? That's a risk! Instead of telling God what you would like to do for him, just make yourself available. Let him do the choosing—of the job, as well as the person. He has an unblemished track record when it comes to matching people to tasks!

Joseph Also Chose: Matthew 1:18–25

In contrast to Mary's youthful exuberance, Joseph was a man of some experience, with an established carpentry business. And a man with a very difficult choice to make. His options were limited. By law he was justified in rejecting Mary in a public divorce, leaving her open to the scorn and censure of the community and getting on with his life. Betrothal could only be broken by death or a divorce before witnesses. He could not avoid it, but he could *soften* it by making it as private as possible and keeping quiet about the details.

Second, he could ignore Mary's pregnancy, go ahead with their plans to marry, and let the gossip roll on by. In a small town, such an action could hurt his reputation and probably his business. It might be difficult for him to fully trust her in years to come. Difficult to accept and raise another man's child. And the child she bore would carry the lifelong stigma of his mother's indiscretion. But they *could* bravely carry on and hope for the best.

Or—and perhaps the hardest choice—he could determine to believe her angel story and stand by her claim of faithfulness. They would be the butt of many coarse jokes, but at least he would be protecting Mary and her child. And, maybe in time, if he told the story enough, he would come to believe it and to trust her again. Losing Mary and starting over would be so hard. No good options, but which of these bad ones should he take?

For a good and righteous man like Joseph, sleep would come hard. In the dark night hours he was still tossing and grieving. *Mary, Mary, why? You I chose of all the girls in this town. I'm not a handsome man, but I would have given you all I had. Was I not enough for you? Am I too old? Did someone you met on your trip steal your heart and soul? Could you not have waited just a few more months?* Late into the night the choice seemed clear. Doubt overcame desire, and he knew that he must end the engagement as gently as possible. Alone on his bed, crushed by loneliness and dreading the morning, he drifted into a troubled sleep.

Sometime before dawn the angel came to him. Essentially, the angel repeated just what Mary had said (Matthew 1:20–21). But somehow it was more believable coming directly from God. Daybreak found Joseph a totally transformed man. The story, which was nonsense to him before, was now fact. The girl he had doubted was pure and trustworthy. The baby that was not his, he now felt compelled to protect and nurture. The people problems were not all solved, but he and Mary would face them together. And surely God, who had sent this child, would bless them and make their way plain.

Early he must be on his way to see Joachim about changing the wedding date. Just a quiet ceremony would do—no feast, few friends. The important thing was, it was time to bring Mary home. A baby was on the way, and they must work this out together. Joachim would understand. But Anne? "I have a feeling this is not the way to be popular with your new mother-in-law," he mumbled, and bounded out the door.

Touch Point

What a difference a night makes! Have you gone to bed on one side of a problem and waked up on the other? Probably it was not an angel or a dream that refocused your mind. More likely it was what Dr. A. W. Tozer termed, "the ministry of the night." When the soul lies crushed in a heap, when all that has brought joy has left or been taken, when there is nothing remaining but God—and he seems to be hiding—we hold to faith. To what we know is right to do....

And then, after sleepless nights and tasteless days, the darkness begins to give way. Dawn tiptoes in and we sense a beginning of God's hope and healing in our broken spirits. The dark night of the soul is passing, and God is still there, we discover, waiting quietly for us to come to the end of ourselves and lean fully on him. Then—and only then—can he use us in a special work.

Chapter 8

Quiet One

Anna, the Prophetess
(Luke 2:22–39)

The first trumpet blast startled Anna out of an uncommonly deep sleep. Usually by the call to prayer she had been up a while to meet the day. Tossing back her shawl cover, she rose and smoothed her dress and hair, shivering against the chill of the spring morning. The great marble stones of the temple walls could hold the night's cold long into the day. Quickly she rolled her mat, stowing it snugly in the corner. Then, wrapping a black shawl over her head and shoulders as befits a widow, she pulled it around her tiny body, reached for her walking stick, and was off to prayer.

The priests had already opened the great temple doors for the day. Moving cautiously along the porch from pillar to pillar, eventually she ventured out into the sunshine of the women's area and looked through the adjoining court toward the temple proper. Lots had been cast, and designated priests were stirring up the coals on the altar of incense, preparing to bless Israel's new day with a sweet offering to the Lord.

Anna loved the temple. So many nights she had prayed long into the darkness, sympathetic Levites eventually found her a corner of one storeroom to call her own. In that little nook she slept and kept the few possessions needed for her uncomplicated life. And though her niece had offered many times to take her in, Anna was content in the temple courts pursuing her life of prayer. David's psalm was the song of her heart also, though few on the outside could understand why.

"One thing I ask of the Lord, this is what I seek: that I may dwell in the house of the Lord all the days of my life, to gaze upon the beauty of the Lord and to seek him in his temple."

Anna spoke with God as others spoke with a good friend.

Outside, vendors were setting up for the day. Stalls were coming alive with conveniences that worshipers might be urged to buy. Lambs bleated in protest, caged doves flapped against their bars, baskets of fruits and skins of new wine were being made ready. The temple had become more a market than a place of worship, thought Anna, shaking her head against that reality. *At least they cannot come inside the sacred area!*

How she wished her people would care more for the prophecies than for the profits. The noise grew steadily as vendor called cheerily to vendor in the early morning sun. Worshipers were beginning to stream through the courtyard on their way to sacrifice. A pair of preoccupied temple guards strolled casually across the porch roof, paying little attention to their charge below. No feast today; things should be uneventful.

Facing the altar, Anna began to pray, hands up, the sun on her back. As she did each morning and each afternoon, Anna prayed for the hope of her people, Israel. For the Light to come on them in the darkness of their oppression. For salvation by the Hand of One who would restore the glory of David's kingdom to greatness. For peace in the land. One by one, close friends—other widows—joined her in prayer. These were the "Quiet in the Land," the holy ones who had dedicated themselves to keeping hope alive in Israel.

At eighty-four years Anna was the eldest woman of the group and its unspoken leader. Her long widowhood had given her a perspective that others struggled to mirror. Sixty lonely years can make a woman bitter, or it can make her deeper. Anna had chosen *deeper* and was at peace with her strange life.

Sarai rushed in with a basket of warm flatbread and a jar of buttermilk to hand her. Anna flushed slightly at the loving care of her friend. "Thank you so much, dear. I'll eat it a bit later, and it will be all I need for the day." Many days no one remembered, and Anna let her prayers be her food. Seeing the basket, a pigeon flew down near her feet, and eyed her knowingly. "O, silly bird, I might have known," she scolded her little friend, tossing him a pinch of bread. "Now, *shoo!* before the whole flock arrives," and she swished him away with her skirt.

More worshipers were coming. Young families with baby boys to dedicate. Older men leading lambs, followed by wives and children toting baskets of grain and the firstfruits of their crops. *The priests will eat well today,* she thought. Anna hoped the offerings came from hearts of devotion and not simply out of duty or custom. Jerusalem was too rich for its own good these days. Social events and politics left little time for the truly spiritual life.

"Well, look there," exclaimed Rachel, motioning toward the south portal. "What is old Simeon doing here so early?" Anna turned to see her aged friend coming across the court, unsteady on his walking stick. The old prophet still came almost every day, weather permitting, but usually a little nearer the afternoon prayers. Sometimes he sat a while with the women, for he too was part of the "Quiet in the Land."

Simeon stopped about midway and scanned the crowd. "Something is on his mind," Anna said with the knowing look of a very old friend. She saw Naomi stop to talk with him and turn away looking surprised.

Rachel also saw, and called out, "Naomi, come and join us." And when she did, Rachel asked, "What is on old Simeon's mind today? He's early."

"Oh, he says the Messiah is coming today," Naomi answered, a little amused. "The Spirit of God told him."

"He *said* that?" Rachel asked, amazed. "Poor old Simeon. I think he is hearing voices again. He so wants salvation in our day that he is imagining it."

"He believes God has told him he won't die until it comes," Miriam added confidentially. "If his Mary were still alive, she would be having a fit, I'll tell you!"

"Hush, all of you," Anna scolded gently. "Show Simeon more respect. He is a godly man and deserves our reverence. For all we know, God *has* told him *exactly* that. Who are we to say?" A guilty quiet fell on the group.

Anna kept watching the old prophet as he searched the faces of all who came through the gate. Abruptly he nodded and shuffled toward one peasant couple. The wife was carrying an infant, and the father held a cage of doves—the offering of the poor. Today, Anna knew, would be purification day—the young mother's reentry into society. Simeon was near enough now to raise a hand of blessing, and the young family stopped, bowing respectfully. Smiling, he reached for the baby. The young mother handed him over carefully, protecting his tiny neck and head. She let go only when the stranger had him safely in the crook of his arm. Perhaps she thought this was part of what was expected of her today, Anna thought.

At that moment Simeon looked deeply into the infant's face, and, with trembling hand raised, broke into loud and joyful praises. "Sovereign Lord, as you have promised, you now may dismiss your servant in peace. For my eyes have seen your salvation, which you have prepared in the sight of all people, a light for revelation to the Gentiles and for glory to your people Israel!"

Holding the child to his breast, Simeon grasped him around the ribs with both hands and raised him high above himself as an offering to the Lord. The anxious mother reached upwards with him, as if to catch her child. *Bless her heart!* Anna said to herself, and left the women to start towards the baby as quickly as an old prophetess could travel.

Simeon lowered the child and began speaking again. "Bless you both," he said, and turned to face the mother. "This child is destined to cause the falling and rising of many in Israel, and to be a sign that will be spoken against, so that the thoughts of many hearts will be revealed. And a sword will pierce your own soul, too." Pride now turned to concern on the face of the child's father, and great fear haunted his mother.

Anna hurried up and took the baby carefully from Simeon's shaking hands. Smiling reassuringly at the new parents, Anna turned to look fast into the tiny face of her Lord. "He's beautiful," she said quietly. "Praise God for his wonderful child! The Son of the Almighty is here with us!" Turning back to her friends, she called out, "Miriam! Sarai! All of you come and see this child! Is this not the Prince of Peace? He is the answer to our prayers! Salvation is near! So near that our children will see it in their day!"

"Bless you," she whispered to the baby's mother, returning the precious bundle to her eager arms.

Behind the Scene
A Study of Luke 2:22–39

Keeping Hope Alive: Luke 2:25–32

Every age must have its Annas and its Simeons—deeply devout men and women who make God's view of history their own, dedicating themselves to earnest prayer that the will of God will be done in his people. In Israel, these people were referred to as the "Quiet in the Land." While the priests were busy slaughtering and roasting lambs, keeping the Old Testament laws of sacrifice, and while the vendors stocked their stalls, hoping to profit from the trappings of the worship system, and while citizens came and went from the temple, fulfilling quickly their obligations to God, the "Quiet in the Land" kept hope alive. If you have not already done so, stop now and read the entire story of Simeon and Anna.

Israel's temple was the heart and soul of the nation. Every Jewish man, (and many women), came there regularly to celebrate feasts and make the required sacrifices of The Law. But, when they had completed their worship, they left Jerusalem to go back to the rest of their lives. To family concerns, neighborhood gossip, paying taxes and running the farm. The "Quiet in the Land," however, stayed behind to study the Scripture's prophecies and pray that Messiah would soon come. That's how Anna spent her life. She had come to have one focus one single purpose. Day and night she kept the doors of heaven vibrating with her knocking, pleading for a Savior, a deliverer, a spiritual leader for her nation. She had lost her life in order to find it.

Praying for the lost of our land is a worthy vocation, but few seek it. It is never popular to be different, even for spiritual reasons. Too much zeal puts people off. And the cost is high. Yet a holy lifestyle is the requisite for an effective life of intercessory prayer. Discouragement sets in when the need for changes in our nation seem to be beyond even the answering power of God. Friends and family seldom understand. Holiness is mistaken for arrogance, and resentment becomes an unspoken response. The life chosen by the *Quiet Ones* is unselfish, sacrificial, misunderstood, and lonely. That is how Anna had chosen to live. Yet surely many who knew her, as they went about their lives and routines, reflected on occasion that it was good that someone—or a few someones—were in touch with God, praying day and night for the nation and the world.

Touch Point

Do you know anyone today who is really attuned to the heartbeat of God? Whose life pays the price to "keep hope alive" regarding the future of the church and the return of the Savior? We must look at our own prayer lives and ask, "Do my concerns go beyond my own household and circle of friends? Have I discovered an eternal view of life and the future? Or am I totally consumed with the living of my life?" Hard questions for women.

Most of us have framed a picture in our minds of the *good life* we seek. Usually it

**includes a comfortable home; healthy, smart
kids; some real friends; a good name; and
enough spiritual life and ministry to round
it all out. Contrast that with Anna's choices:
no home, no close family, little or no social
life—just *prayer*—night and day. How does
that contrast strike you?**

**All are not called to separate, to live in the
temple in the seclusion of extreme spirituality, so to speak. But all are called to study the
Word of God and keep moving toward having the mind of Christ. First John 2:15–17
continues to be a flashlight shining on life's
pathway.**

In our family, the "Quiet One" was my husband's
maiden Aunt Mildred. She was the woman of prayer
and fasting for us. Throughout our ministry in the
pastorate we knew she prayed daily for us, and while
her spirituality was sometimes chafing, we respected
her greatly. One morning we were facing a particularly
troubling problem at the church. Feelings were raw, and
any decision was likely to rankle one group or another.
When Jack left for the office, I called long distance to
Aunt Mildred and asked her to pray that God would
work things out among his people. She listened, asking
enough questions to make her prayers wise, and we hung
up. At about seven that evening our phone rang, and
Aunt Mildred was on the line. "I have prayed all day
and fasted two meals. Now I need to know what God
has done today." She both sacrificed for us and held *us*

accountable. She was *our* Anna until late in her life, as long as God kept her able.

The Gift of Prophecy: Luke 2:36–38

Although we have tied the passages about Anna to the previous story of Simeon, these three little verses are the sum total of our direct information about one of the fascinating women in the gospel account. She was Anna, the Prophetess. In addition to her life of holiness and prayer, she had been given the gift of prophecy. What did that mean in the female gender?

There were several prophetesses in the Bible—both Old Testament and New. Recall Moses' sister Miriam in Exodus 15:20 and Deborah, the Judge, in Judges 4:4–5. Philip is credited with four maiden daughters who prophesied in Acts 2:8–9. And the promises of Acts 2:17–18 include daughters with sons, and women along with men who will prophecy.

> "In the last day, God says, I will pour out my Spirit on all people. Your sons and daughters will prophesy... Even on my servants, both men and women, I will pour out my Spirit in those days and they will prophesy."

None of the lists of spiritual gifts in the Bible deny women the gift of speaking for God. (See Romans 12:4–8, 1 Corinthians 12:4–11). While they were far fewer, and less well-known, women prophets—identified in the Word by that name—are a notable part of scripture story.

Prophets and prophetesses spoke for God to the people. They received messages from God and gave them to the people. Sometimes they spoke of the future, but more often gave insights for the present day. Where priests were to concern themselves with sacrifices, prophets focused on behavior and ethics, on love for God, and on obedience to his Word. They were a purifying force in society. Simeon and Anna have the distinction of being the first prophets to speak "on the record" after the birth of Jesus.

Anna's words came out of a life of fasting, prayer, and holy living. She kept distractions out of her life and thus was able—probably alone, in the quiet night hours—to hear and discern the Voice of God to her heart. Today we might look for her in a convent or a monastery, and observe her life with awe.

A dear and close friend, General Robbie Risner, who served as a Prisoner of War in Vietnam for seven years, tells of hearing the Voice of God in the solitude. Much of his time was spent locked in solitary confinement, without significant human communication. He used the time to exercise and pray mostly. The cell size limited his exercise, but it could not restrict his conversations with God. At times he had experiences of hearing God speak audibly to prepare him for a coming encounter with enemy prison guards. Once liberated and back in the United States, he told us, the distractions of life closed in, and he found the Voice was not often heard in that same way.

Touch Point

Dare we bring up the discipline of prayer? It is such a struggle for most of us! Yet it is the foundation from which every spiritual gift develops and matures. How does a busy person living with the distractions of this life find time to speak to God, let alone listen to him?

Jesus caught time in the late evenings, after the crowds had dispersed (Mark 6:45–46), and in the early mornings, before his Disciples were awake (Mark 1:35). He prayed when exhaustion had overtaken everyone else (Matthew 26:40–41). Paul found plenty of time—after he was put in prison. There he prayed day and night (Colossians 1:9). Secretly we have to be happy that God has not chosen such desperate situations to discipline us in prayer. But it *could* happen!

Mostly we pray on the run. And that is not bad, but neither is it enough. One little trick could probably revolutionize our prayer lives—and *today!* We could turn off the TV for an hour. Or just sneak away while the family is entertained. Catch an hour alone with the Lord—without commercials!

What does one do before God for an hour? Pray through a psalm. Begin a journal of requests and personal growth. Make a list of persons for whom you need to intercede. And listen! God is speaking through his Word

and through the meditations of our hearts. Did you find an hour is not enough? Maybe you'll need to skip two programs!

The Gift of Aging: Another Look at Luke 2:36–38

So many people fear the natural process called "aging." Nervous jokes are made about the alternatives, but few consider aging a gift. True, it has its downside. All the bad habits of our younger years come home to roost with age. All the weak links in our gene pool manifest themselves. But look at a few of the benefits that offset these challenges.

Anna was eighty-four years old. That is beyond what most term "active senior adult," and well into the "frail elderly" category. No doubt she had aches and pains, and perhaps some serious health concerns. Could she see and hear well? Did she have all her teeth? Was her memory playing tricks on her? How severe was her arthritis on that cold temple morning? We cannot know. Yet somehow, over and above the normal problems of aging, Anna had managed to discover several priceless treasures in her life. Look at them closely.

The first was *meaning*—the desire to be part of the will and work of God. While younger people went about making a living, Anna had a life! To be happy, a life must stay bigger than we are. It must tie onto something that is going forward, something that will outlive us. Something that will make life better for others. If not, life is over before it is over. At eighty-four Anna's life was far from over. She was putting to use all the richness of her maturity and (we think) loving it. She was not just an old lady in the temple; she was Anna, the Prophetess—a title of respect.

Anna's second treasure was *friends*. She was a recognized fixture at the temple. They had apparently accommodated to her by providing some way for her to live on the grounds. And when she recognized, with Simeon's help, the Christ Child, she turned to speak to others who shared her life's passion (notice verse 38b). Anna was part of a group of holy women and men who served at the temple every day. She was out with people, experiencing the give-and-take of conversation and caring. Old friends who have grown together over the years, sharing sorrows and joys, raising their children together, burying their husbands together—these are the best kind. For all the cold marble around her, life was warm for Anna. She belonged.

Sorrow and tragedy had not worn her down. Anna's third treasure was *contentment*—being at peace with who she was. Most women of her day, as in ours, grew up desiring a husband, a home, and a family. Anna had been a bride once, but her short marriage lasted just seven years (if we read Scripture correctly). Then sorrow came, and her husband died. We know nothing of the details, or whether she had children or other living family. At eighty-four she is bound to have buried most of the people she loved. Who knows what other heartaches had driven her to the temple to pray? She must have felt safe there, protected by sturdy stone columns. She must have found God very present there, for at some point she abandoned all other attempts at life and settled down to be who she was: one lady alone in the world, holding tight to the Hand of God. Age helps us drop our pretenses and adjust our expectations. Being a widowed holy woman was all right with Anna. She had grown to love her life.

Touch Point

What wonderful gifts! Meaning in life, friends to share life with, contentment with our place in life.... It recalls the words of Whittier in a little-sung hymn:

Dear Lord and Father of mankind,
forgive our foolish ways.
Reclothe us in our rightful mind;
in purer love thy service find;
in deeper rev'rence, praise.

Drop thy still dews of quietness,
'till all our strivings cease.
Take from our souls the strain and stress,
and let our ordered lives confess,
the beauty of thy peace.

Part 2

WOMEN TOUCHED BY JESUS' EARLY MINISTRY

Chapter 4

Valued

The Samaritan Woman
(John 4:4–42)

The half-mile walk to draw water always seemed endless on a summer day. Tamara pulled her veil farther down over her eyes to shade them from the glaring sun. Down the road she could hear a band of travelers coming toward her. Squinting into the noonday she tried to count. There must be nine, maybe ten of them, all men, laughing and talking loudly. *Jews, no doubt, shortcutting on their way north to Galilee. Funny how they love our roads, but hate our people,* she thought, resentfully. No Samaritan for miles around was happy to see a Jew coming—unless, of course, he had money in his purse and needed food and drink or lodging.

As the men neared, Tamara could tell that they were Galileans. Their accents were unmistakable. Seeing her, they fell silent, as if they had secrets to keep. Tamara stepped off the pathway and looked away, resting her water jar on a rock as they passed. None spoke—no surprise to her. Jewish men never spoke to a woman in public—especially a Samaritan woman—especially *her.*

As she heard their voices begin again she lifted her clay pot to her shoulder to resume the walk to the well. A snide laugh was carried on the breeze, and Tamara glanced back, just in time to see two of the men gesturing toward her. Their eyes barely met, and all quickly turned away. She had seen that look before—often. The knowing look of judgment that men are so prone to give. *They don't even know me and they have decided about me,* she thought bitterly. *What gives them the right to treat me as though I am no more than dirty linen or a broken dish?*

Old angers rose up inside her and, try as she would, she could not put their scorn out of her mind. *Why do they not see that my life is what it is because of men just like them? Men who took what they wanted, and cast me aside like a broken sandal.* She was walking faster now, distracted by her rage, running from familiar feelings of shame. With one corner of her veil she pressed back tears and missed seeing a loose rock in the path. Stumbling, she almost dropped the empty water jar, then kicked at the stone angrily. Her throat tightened and, from some place deep in her soul, tears rolled down her face, as once again the demons took control.

Flashes of memory played in her mind. She was just a girl, working alone with her brother in the field.

Valued

One minute they were children playing, the next she was forced by his clumsy passions. Pleas to her mother brought an impatient brush-off. "Don't be caught alone where he can get at you." How can a girl protect herself from a brother four years older and stronger? It happened again and again, and no one seemed to care.

Then she was barely a teen, too young to marry but eager to leave home. At the first offer her father gave her away gladly, and she was wed to the household of Ezra, a widower with five children and a hard-to-please mother. "Don't expect any special privileges here," Monica warned. "I'm first in line, and my grandchildren with me. You take what's left…and be happy with it. They don't make girls like my generation any more." Tamara settled in to the menial chores, doing what Monica directed, available when Ezra beckoned. Life was drudgery at best, slavery at worst. She hoped in time that a baby would bring joy to her life—someone to love and need her. But God did not send one. Monica mocked her and Ezra was not pleased. He took to venting his displeasure in drunken bursts of rage. Caught in a downward spiraling despair, one day she slipped away, running through the fields to another village.

Seeking work in an inn outside the town, she found a raucous keep who asked, "Girl, can you dance? My customers will pay well for a clever dancer." Hungry and alone, Tamara did not have much left to lose. She tried, and, to her delight, was the best feature of the evening. It felt very good to be valued for something she did well. No one asked where she had come from or why she was there. "Dance, girl, dance," was all they said. And the coins flew, making the innkeeper happy. After the dancing there were men who would pay even more for her company through the night. There are always men who will pay—with money their wives never see.

Abram came from that crowd. He was a trader from Damascus who promised her the moon. Tired from months of serving whoever happened by, Tamara went north with him to Syria. It sounded romantic—travel, escape, new people who did not know her past. But things are seldom what a girl hopes they will be. Abram's family never accepted this "foreign wife," and he was away from Damascus most of the time. When he came home, he believed what they told him, and, oftener than not, Tamara's welcome was a beating. Something deep inside told her she was worth more than life was giving back. By dark of night she left, heading south for lack of another plan. Three nights she walked and cried and thought, and slept by day, eventually arriving back at the inn and her old job. She was in a box with no way out.

Tamara shook off her sadness and shifted the water jar to her other shoulder. Strange how the horrors of other days can never be fully put to death, though years pass. Jacob's well was in sight now. She lingered a moment in the sparse shade of a scrub Juniper tree. Wisps of clouds were gathering over the holy mountain, promising some relief from the sun overhead. Tamara slipped her veil down around her shoulders and fell into a few more minutes of reverie. *Well, that accounts for Ezra and Abram—and good riddance to both,* she thought. Samuel was another story, another kind of man. Samuel was good to her, and though she had vowed that there never would be a husband number three, he won her by his bright humor and kind smile. And she was so hungry for some joy in her life! On a night of too much wine and too little sense, she consented to marry him.

Things were good for a while. She had always thought that marriage would have made it if Samuel had lived. One winter the fever swept through their village, and though she nursed him desperately, death took him. Tamara was left alone in their tiny, one-room house—but not for long. Samuel's brother, Seth, soon came and claimed the property for the family...*and her,* as a part of it. Seth was not the fun-loving man Samuel had been. His house was run with a strong arm, and his sons were sassy and rude. She soon took advantage of the back door. He never bothered to come looking for her. The house was all he had really wanted.

It was time to go home to Sychar. Her mother was old and alone now, and Tamara could be of help. Poor Mother—she died never acknowledging her part in the whole mess. Her refusal to intervene in those ruined childhood years was the beginning of Tamara's tragic life of pain, bad decisions, struggle for survival. Sighing deeply, in spite of herself, she gathered up her resignation, along with the water jug, to begin the last of her trip to Jacob's well.

Life has some justice, she thought to herself as she walked. Even a life as soiled as hers. In time her mother died, leaving her the house, the goat, and the garden. It was humble, but she could manage on it. For the most part Tamara lived quietly, keeping to herself. She was blessed with good neighbors in Micah and Mary, and grew to love them both. Many cool evenings were spent in conversation under the Acacia tree that grew between their houses. Mary was a frail and sickly lady, but gentle of spirit and words. Micah was a devoted husband who waited on her from early morning 'til late evening. Tamara often fixed extra porridge and bread to take them, so they would be saved from the daily chore of cooking. But despite all these efforts, Mary worsened, and in the middle of winter six years ago, she died of the cough.

Micah was so sad. Tamara barely saw him for weeks. But in time he came to sit beneath the Acacia again, and one evening she joined him. Their friendship grew into love—the love of mature people whose lives have been deepened by sorrow. When he invited her into his house, she quietly accepted. She had never been more at home. They had several happy years before he had died—just a year ago now. He had taken her heart with him, and now she had only to live out her time, warmed by the memory of his love.

Tamara herself was too old and too wise now to want a man. Five were enough and too much. Micah's older brother, Thad, had come to live with them the year before he died. Tamara had been happy to let him have the tiny room on their roof and take meals with them. He was a simple-minded man—unschooled, but willing to help with the goats and the garden. He needed Tamara to cook for him, and she welcomed his help with the chores, so the arrangement continued after Micah was gone. There was comfort in not being totally alone. It was because of Thad that she was making this extra jaunt to the well. He had accidentally fallen against the half-full jar and upset it, spilling the water they needed for the night. To calm him, she had insisted she needed some exercise, and an unexpected trip to the well would be just the thing. Now she was nearly there.

Looking up, Tamara was startled by a stranger sitting on the rock trough beside the well. *Another Jew,* she thought with disdain, only this time his shawl told her he was probably a rabbi. She sighed uneasily. If men were quick to judge her, how much more would this holy man of The Law? Beside him were travel bags and backpacks. Perhaps, she surmised, he was keeping the duffle for the traveling band she had passed on the road earlier.

Circling to the far side of the well, she tied her leather pouch to the rope and tossed it down. Cool, damp currents rose upward from stony depths and bathed her sunburned cheeks. She kept her eyes on the bucket as it made the hundred-foot drop and splashed into the gathered waters below. Silence built like a wall. She could feel the stranger's eyes without looking up. Quickly, again and again, she drew up her bucket, working to fill her jar and get back on her way quickly. Both would be more comfortable when she was not sharing his space.

"Will you give me a drink?" the stranger asked quietly. Tamara pulled up the last bucketful, met his eyes, and walked slowly to where he rested. As he took the water and drank deeply, she could not help asking him the obvious question.

"You are a Jew and I am a Samaritan. You are a man and I am a woman. How can you ask for water from me?" *Most men,* she thought, *would consider themselves unfit for worship if they had spoken to a Samaritan woman, let alone taken a drink from her container.*

Wiping his wet beard on his sleeve, Jesus smiled and set out to explain.

Behind the Scene
A Study of John 4:4–42

How Did John Know?

In our earlier story we saw that Luke alone of the gospel writers told of the angels coming to Zechariah and Mary, explained the census of Caesar Augustus, and slipped in the temple vignette of old Simeon and Anna. So John alone saved for us many treasured stories such as this one. Traditional wisdom of early fathers assumed that John, having seen the accounts of Mark and Matthew, set about to supplement them with parts of Jesus' ministry they had not included. That explanation is as good as any available to us, and better than some.

It is because of John that we have details about Jesus' first meeting with some of his Disciples at the revival of John the Baptist in Judea. John alone records the first miracle—water made into wine at the Cana wedding feast. And without John's gospel, we would not know about Nicodemus' secret nighttime visit—or his part in the burial of Jesus. John has given us treasures indeed!

But how did John alone know this verbatim account of Jesus' encounter with the woman from Sychar? Had he remained behind to be company and protection for Jesus, and so been witness to the event? Perhaps when the Sychar revival was over and the troop resumed their journey to Galilee, John and Jesus talked, and John remembered Christ's recounting of this encounter. Because the record was included and preserved for us through the hovering safekeeping of God's Spirit, we know it to be history. Stop and read her story, soaking in all the amazing truths and details, now.

Getting on the Map: John 4:4–6

Israel is about 120 miles long, north to south. Jesus had been in the south, Judea, and wanted to return home to the north, Galilee. The middle forty miles of Israel was occupied by the Samaritans—age-old adversaries of the Jews north and south of it. Many Jews refused to travel through Samaria, choosing instead to cross from Judea, over the Jordan River, and hike up the east side until they could re-cross into Galilee. The hatred of these two cultures was mutual and had very deep roots. How can we understand it?

Reach way back to the time when the Northern Kingdom of Israel was overrun by Assyria, about 722 B.C. The vacuum, left when Assyria carried the choice residents of Israel away captive, was later filled with imported foreigners, transplanted there in an attempt to wipe any memory of Israel off the face of history. Of course they brought with them other gods, and in time settled in and married the left-behind Jews, creating the mixed race that came to be known as *Samaritans.*

The Southern Kingdom of Judah endured another several generations, until it, too, fell in about 586 B.C., and its best citizens were carried captive into Babylon in waves of removal. Daniel and Ezekiel were among those taken. The mixed-race Samaritans and others moved southward to fully possess the land.

Take a memory-step forward from there to about 440 B.C., when Ezra and Nehemiah returned with many southern Jews to rebuild the sacred temple and the wall of Jerusalem. The Samaritans, having enjoyed over 200 years of possession (how old is the United States?), fought every Jewish attempt to reclaim their Promised Land. The Jews, having endured painful captivity because of their former sins of intermarriage and idolatry, wanted no part of cohabiting with these heathens who worshiped Jehovah, along with other gods. The Samaritans were driven north, away from the Jerusalem area, but held the in-between land known in Jesus' day as Samaria.

Now the groups coexisted in the Roman peace, but never forgot their enmity. Neither missed a chance to insult the other. The Jews, viewing Samaritans not as relatives but as Gentiles, considered the land, the people, and even having conversation with them as unclean. At times in history Jews would not even eat food handled by Samaritans, and any contact with them made a Jew unfit for worship. The Samaritans, disenfranchised from the temple at Jerusalem but considering themselves children of Abraham and Moses, built a competing temple at Mt. Gerizim, near Sychar. The common ground between them—their ancestry through Abraham, their history from the days when Isaac and Jacob grazed and watered their flocks in the area, their worship based on the Law of Moses—this was considered void by the Jews. And peace cannot survive in the face of such arrogance—in Jesus' day or in ours.

Why then, did Jesus take his band through Samaria, instead of the more pleasant, eastern route? John 4:4 tells us he *"had to."* Whether it was a decision based on time—the route through Samaria was direct and shorter—or on desire to evangelize, we can only wonder. Arriving about noon (six hours after sunrise) he was hot, hungry, and exhausted. The well at the road fork was a welcome oasis. Those who know tell us this well, dug by Jacob's men hundreds of years before, was over a hundred feet deep—perhaps 130 feet. Speculate a minute on how they bored through limestone to water with no power tools. The well had been cooling travelers and supplying area residents for over 1500 years! Leaving Jesus to rest in view of the holy mountain, the Disciples started the half-mile trail into town, in the hope that some greedy Samaritan would sell them food.

Breaking Tradition: John 4:7–9

Probably all the duffle was stacked around Jesus, and in it there may have been a leather bucket or two. Maybe Jesus, after walking all morning, was too physically spent to look for it. Or maybe he saw an opportunity that was too good to pass up. Some would have considered the woman (she had a name, but John didn't reveal it, so we have given her a lovely one, "Tamara") to be a tough case for witnessing. As it turned out, Jesus had no trouble at all getting through to her. The need for a drink was his entry.

Rejection was a common companion of this woman. She sensed it immediately. Men did not speak to women in public. Jewish men did not speak to her at all. Jews were uppity toward Samaritans. As she sized-up the situation, this would be a silent sharing of space. She no doubt set about doing her task quickly. The very fact that she had chosen Jacob's well, instead of nearer springs, may reveal that she was avoiding contact with people—specifically the town women, who were critical of her past and her lifestyle.

But Jesus chose to speak to her. What is contained in those six words, "Will you give me a drink?" *Kindness*: Had he been arrogant or rude she probably would not have complied with his request. *Hope*: She was thirsty to be accepted and valued, and here was someone who could break the glass wall of tradition. Perhaps he would help her feel better about herself. *Trust*: Someone had a critical need that she could fill. He trusted her to respond with decency. She trusted him and moved to within arm's length. Did their eyes meet? Did he smile and thank her? Did she sit on the well to rest as he drank from her goatskin bucket? That may be too much to assume. It was, after all, only the First Century. But we can see that Jesus reached across barriers of race, gender, language, religion, and disgrace in order to take the bucket from her hands.

Touch Point

We don't have to go to Samaria to feel the awkwardness of being near someone who is

not like us—not accepted in our world. Reverse the situation in today's society. Imagine finding yourself in the company of a man of another racial group—one of a standing that would be thought much higher or lower than yourself. A distinguished Ph.D., perhaps, or an unkempt street person. Maybe someone wearing an Eastern turban? How desperate would you or I need to be to open up a dialogue with him—or to ask him for help? How close to the top of our conversation would spiritual topics be? Would we call this a witnessing situation?

Take one further step. Would we go out of our way to find such a person? To set up a conversation? How does one know when God is leading her to step several paces out of her comfort zone and find an unlikely person with a spiritual need? Where would we find common ground for such a conversation? What kind of expression would show on our faces and in our voices? What risks would need to be considered?

One more thought. You and I likely know a Tamara—a woman thirsty to be valued, waiting and hoping for a way back into the mainstream of acceptance and vital faith. God can show us the common ground that will put us within arm's length of her need.

All Those Excuses: John 4:10–26

Jesus made his offer of "living water," fresh-running water that would quench her heart's longing forever. It took a little discussion before they could get on the same wavelength. She was thinking *physical* thirst, and he was talking about her thirst for God. She was thinking a *Samarian* mountain, and he was talking a heavenly Kingdom. And when she realized the conversation was becoming personal, she responded with excuses and shallow debate.

"How can you give me water when you have no bucket?" "Who do you think you are—a prophet?" "Do you think your church is better than mine?" "Do you think there is only one way to God?"

Then he did it. Jesus stopped the word games and laid bare her sinful past. It must have taken her breath away. "You have had five husbands, and the man you live with now is not your husband." A clinical psychologist would have spent hours of cautious probing before that lady could admit out loud all the stuff in her sad life. All the bad marriages and affairs, and everything before, after and in between. It would have come at the cost of many tears, excuses, and tirades of anger toward those who had led her astray. Don't try this at home! Only Jesus could have done it this way—no one else could have instinctively known and cut to the truth as this God/Man could do.

Touch Point

How does it feel when we realize God sees through all our excuses and rationalizations and knows who we really are? The good and the ugly, the motives and the desires, yesterday and today, without varnish or whitewash or designer clothes? Is it disconcerting to be so totally uncovered? Is it not terribly reassuring to be loved in spite of the truth? "The more we are forgiven, the more we love," Jesus told his Pharisee friend (Luke 7:42–43).

Does it do anything for your prayer life when you know you can drop all pretense because Jesus already knows the truth about you and accepts you as you are? Even more—that he feels you still have something to offer him in his work?

How hard is it to transfer that acceptance to others? What does it take for us to try to love as God loves? Can we discover another person's weaknesses, her past story, her sins, and value her anyway? Why is that hard? What can make us let go of critically judging others, while overlooking our *own* failures? It may be the "mote vs. beam" thing Jesus taught in Matthew 7:1–5. But God has never given us the right to judge—just the right to love. Oh, Tamara's story touches us where we hurt!

Free to Be Loved: John 4:27–42

The Disciples suffered from the same myopic condition as we do! So focused on themselves were they, they could not see the value of those close by. All the way to town and back, and they never let the *cat out of the bag* that Jesus was sitting half-a-mile away. Within a few feet of the woman, and they could not see that she was worth saving. Ready to spread the picnic, but choking on the bread of kindness. How blind we Christians be! So tangled in the physical world and dull to the spiritual. How many opportunities have we walked right past—even today?

But "Tamara" was feeling free for the first time in years. She left everything at the well that day—her water jar, her drawing bucket, and her shame. Feet flying, veil trailing like a banner, can you see her running to free the very town that had held her down and out most of her life? So thirsty were they all for the quenching, refreshing truth that they traipsed the dusty half mile behind the most questionable woman in town—and found the very Person of Christ sitting on their village well.

Then Jesus went to town, followed by his amazed, reluctant Disciples, and the joyful revival lasted two more days. "Outcasts and sinners will enter the kingdom before religious folks," Jesus had predicted (Matthew 21:31b). And right here, in the middle of Samaria, he drew them all a picture of this truth in the sand.

Chapter 5

Caught By Change

Peter's Mother-in-Law
(Mark 1:14–39)

Miriam tasted the steaming stew, dropped in a little more salt and cumin, then gave the pot a good stirring. Pulling it carefully onto fresh coals, she turned to check the crock of boiling figs beside it. Finding them done, she set them off the fire to cool.

In her mind she ran through the menu once more. Peter wanted everything to be right with Jesus coming to dinner. The stew was about done and the figs cooling. She had mixed the wine, and the table was set. She counted the loaves from her early baking. Yes, there were probably enough, even for this crowd. Anyway, it was too late to bake more now. Cheese and olives were already set out. Peter had milked the ewes before leaving for synagogue, and the milk was cooling in two crocks beside the table. She'd prepared the squash and onions yesterday, and that—along with a generous platter of salted fish—should be plenty. *We have to serve fish in a fisherman's house,* she mused. Company dinners were common at Peter and Andrew's house, but usually Mama Esther headed up the preparations. Today she was too ill.

Confident that things were as ready as possible, Miriam stepped into the back room to check on her ailing mother. Esther had been sick with a high fever for nearly two days, quite sick, and Miriam was growing concerned. Finding her awake, Miriam whispered, "How are you feeling, Mama?"

Esther turned on her mat to face her pregnant daughter. "Not well, dear. I'm so sorry I can't get up and help you with the meal. Of all times for me to be sick! Is everything going all right?"

"Everything's fine, Mama. Don't worry. You taught me well." Miriam wiped her hands on her bulging apron. "I miss your help, but I want you to rest and get better." She walked to the mat, stooped down, and felt her mother's face with her wrist. "You are really burning up with fever, Mama. Are you getting worse?"

"I can't tell, Miriam. This fever is just miserable. One minute I'm hot and the next I'm cold, and I ache all over. Good as the food smells, I can't bear to think of eating a thing." Esther reached for her daughter's hand. "Did you tie the knife to the thorn bush for me?"

"Yes, Mother. I did that yesterday when you asked. I tied it with the braid of your hair."

"An iron knife, like the rabbis say?" Esther persisted.

"Yes, Mama. Grandfather's butcher knife. And I said the Scripture words."

"Then, all we can do is wait it out," she sighed with resignation.

"Would you like for me to open the shutters and let in some fresh air, Mama? It's stuffy in here." Miriam moved toward the small, shuttered vent.

"No, dear. The draft makes me chilly, and the light is too bright. I just need to rest. Maybe the knife cure will work and I'll feel better in a few hours." Esther pulled the covers around her shoulders and closed her eyes.

Miriam studied her mother with a worried face, tucked the blanket in around her feet, and smoothed back her damp, gray hair. "How about some more herb tea? I have hot water, and can make it in just a jiffy."

"No, dear. Thanks. Nothing right now." Esther didn't even open her eyes. "Just let me sleep."

"I only wish I could help you, Mama. I hate for you to be so sick. Salome will be here as soon as Sabbath service is over. She's a pretty good healer. Maybe she will know something we can do to get you well quicker." She patted her mother's hand and turned to go.

"Just go tend to your company. I'll lie here and rest."

Loudly through the door came Salome's voice. "Miriam? Esther? Who is home?"

"Come in, Salome." Miriam called as she hurried toward the front of the house. "Shalom. I'm so glad you are here," she said, kissing her neighbor and friend. "Mama is sick with the burning fever—so very sick. Come and look at her, and tell me what to do to get her well."

"Yes, I heard it at the well earlier. And I saw the knife on the thorn bush outside. Here…" Salome shoved a basket and bundles into Miriam's hands. "I brought along the extra bread and some fresh plums picked just this morning. They are very ripe. I hope you can use them. Now, where is our Esther?"

"In the other room resting. She is so very hot. Go right in, Salome, and thank you for the bread and plums. I was a little short on bread. I'm not quite as good as Mama at getting this company thing done." Salome tiptoed into the adjoining room, and Miriam walked over to add the bread to her own basket. Finding an empty bowl, she arranged the plums for the center of the table.

"Esther?" Salome queried softly. "I heard at the well that you were ill." As she talked she bent to feel her friend's face. "Oh, my! You do have a case of it!" she blurted out, alarmed.

"I guess I'm a mess," Esther answered, rousing slightly. "Is Sabbath service done already?

"No, dear. Jehovah will have to understand. When I heard you were sick, I got Zebedee and the boys off to service and came right over here. I thought Miriam would welcome some help, but it looks like she has everything about ready." Salome tested her friend's brow a second time, then turned to call through the doorway. "Miriam, bring your mother a cup of herb tea with honey. She must *drink* something to get over this fever."

Esther rolled to face her old friend. "Salome, I hear your James and John have decided to leave Capernaum with this Jesus prophet. Our Simon and Andrew are going, too. And Abigail's Philip, and maybe some others. What do you make of it?" She tried not to betray her deep concern.

"I'm sick over it," wailed Salome. "Just absolutely sick. Actually, I worried in the bed while Zebedee slept. I don't know what Zeb will do. I guess he will have to hire extra hands. But at his age, it is sad for him to lose his boys. He lives and breathes for those boys." She shook her head sadly.

"Do you know much about this Jesus? I've heard good news and bad."

Miriam came in with the tea and some bread, lifting her mother's head while she sipped the drink. "Try to eat some of Salome's good rye bread, Mama. You need to eat something to get well."

Salome's voice filled the silence. "I heard he was kicked out of the synagogue in Nazareth just last week. The people there almost killed him, they were so angry. That's the bad news, I guess. But James and John say he has been doing miracles of healing and that his teaching is amazing. I just don't know what to think, Esther. Right now..." She paused, searching to moderate her words, "I'm not convinced."

Esther sipped the tea quietly. "It's hard to know," she said.

Miriam picked up the thought. "Peter told us the story of making wine in Cana. Andrew says they spent a whole day with Jesus down at the spring where John is baptizing. John seems fully convinced that he is the promised Messiah. You two must not fret so," she consoled, settling her mother and adjusting the covers again. "Peter and James and the others—they are smart men. They won't run off after just any traveling preacher. They are totally convinced that he is the Messiah who will set up the new kingdom. We will all miss them, of course, but what choice do we have but to let them go and find out? The other wives I've talked to feel that way, too. Anyway, they will be in and out."

"Well, I hope you are right," Salome responded quietly. "I never did agree with a man leaving his parents and his family to go off after religion. And with your baby almost due! But maybe this Jesus is more than the others were." She rose to go toward the family room but turned back to her friend. "They claim this Jesus is a miracle-worker and a healer. *Who knows,* Esther? Maybe he will cure your fever."

"We could ask him, Mama," Miriam added hopefully. "It never hurts to ask."

Behind the Scene
A Study of Mark 1:14–39

What Do We Know of the Wives and Mothers?

Actually very little. The Bible only gives us stingy glimpses of the families of the Disciples. Verses like Luke 8:1–3, Mark 15:40–41 and 16:1, Luke 23:55–24:1 and 10, John 19:25–27, and Acts 1:12–14, all give us fascinating clues about the women who were part of Jesus' ministry. We know, of course, that Jesus' mother was still living, and that she sometimes traveled with the group. She was present at the Cross and at Pentecost. Salome, wife of Zebedee and the mother of James and John, seems also to have traveled some with the Disciples (see Matthew 20:20–28) and was involved in activities at the Crucifixion and burial. Now this little vignette about Peter's family, along with Paul's offhand comment in 1 Corinthians 9:5, causes us to know that Peter had a wife and a mother-in-law who was, in some way, part of his household.

To state the obvious, all the disciples had mothers, and some—perhaps most—of these were still alive at the time Jesus organized his staff. We can never know how many had wives, sisters, and in-laws, but it is safe to assume that a number of families, and extended families were affected and disrupted when Jesus called out twelve men to prepare to do his work. We will meet some of these again in later chapters.

A Far-Reaching Decision: Mark 1:14–20

The events leading up the Jesus' calling the fishermen to become his Disciples must be pieced together from all the gospel accounts. John alone tells us of the very significant two days in Judea at the time of Jesus' baptism, when John the Baptizer introduced Jesus to some of his own disciples (see John 1:19–51). John's affirmation of Jesus caused these eager seekers to ask for a meeting with him. The meeting turned into an hours-long get-acquainted session. Involved in this were Andrew, Simon Peter, Philip, Nathaniel, and one other man—probably John, son of Zebedee. Jesus spoke of a new Kingdom—God's true kingdom. They came away impressed—and excited!

Following that meeting, Jesus was led by the Spirit into the temptation period, when much about his coming ministry became clearer in his mind. After that, according to most chronologies, he and some of his early Disciples returned to Galilee via Cana. There they witnessed his first miracle, the turning-of-water-into-wine sign. Other miracles and teachings followed, many of which were witnessed by the growing band.

Then, a setback. Just before officially calling the fishermen, Jesus returned to his home in Nazareth and was thoroughly misunderstood and rejected by the townsfolk. Taking offense at his teachings, which seemed too complimentary of the Gentiles, they herded him off to a cliff and threatened him with death. Only God's direct intervention saved the day (see Luke 4:14–30).

So by the time he splashed along the shore of Galilee and called his four friends out of their boats several weeks had passed, and Jesus was quite well known to the Disciples. Anticipation and vision for the new Kingdom had been building, and these were some very excited young men. Can you read that in John 1:49–51? Israel was an occupied nation, longing to rebuild the glory days of David and Solomon. Jesus promised hope, and they wanted in on the ground floor of whatever this start-up company was to become.

And how was the news received by these barely visible wives, parents, and in-laws? Galilee was not large, and news of Jesus was traveling fast. It isn't far-fetched to assume the stories of his miracles, his teachings, and his confrontations, had preceded him to town. What was this mother-in-law to believe? A mother whose daughter was about to be left behind—perhaps with children on the way, or already in hand, to be cared for? The older generation takes to change more slowly, and for good reason. They are wiser, more protective, more rooted into daily life. They have seen quick decisions hurt many people and have made serious mistakes of their own. They appreciate the value of the *tried-and-true*. Possibly Peter's family responded in some of these ways.

Touch Point

Perhaps it is the role of parent-aged people to curb the tides of change—to hold the beachhead of achievements past. But the time comes when change happens—with or without us—and we have no choice but to make it work. Jobs play out, children move away, friends pass on, doctors retire, technology replaces familiar systems, new laws are passed, health problems arise. Outside we make the needed adjustments. Inside we may be in a pitched battle with anger, fear, grief, and confusion, trying desperately to find our new footing.

It is often hard to sort out the "why" of our feelings. In private moments or with trusted friends, we ask ourselves the hard questions. *Am I simply holding to comfort, or guarding a value worth keeping? Am I*

protecting myself while holding others back?
Is desire for personal control or power driving
me, or am I confident that I am in God's will?
Am I fighting God instead of moving with him?
The questions do not become easier as we get
older. They should keep us on our knees.

Setting Up in Capernaum: Mark 1:21–28

Capernaum became the group's headquarters because the town citizens there were open to Jesus' new teachings and witnessed his wonderful works. He showed himself to be Lord over demons—something not seen before. The work of historians such as Alfred Edersheim explains why this was so amazing. People of that day believed demons to be in every rock and bush, and in the air around them—by the thousands! Most illness was attributed to them. Primitive, first-century medicine had no way to treat demon possession. Priests attempted spiritual exorcisms with elaborate preparations. Jesus, by contrast, simply spoke, and the demons obeyed. Incredible!

Finding acceptance here in Capernaum, Jesus visited often, giving rise to the idea that Peter and Andrew's home near the synagogue may have been his guest quarters. People certainly knew to find him there (Mark 1:32). It is of interest to us that Peter's parents are not mentioned here, but his mother-in-law is present. The gospel writers did not tell us her name—or the name of her daughter—but we have chosen good Jewish names for them to help them jump off the page a little. This, again, is a case where we have only three verses (29–31) in which to find our story. Read them carefully so you will correctly sort the facts from conjecture.

Touch Point

This "Esther" was a good woman. She opened her home to the Lord and his work. She got up from a sickbed ordeal in order to use her gifts in his service. She gave up her son-in-law and assisted her daughter in the new life they had chosen.

Consider what she would have missed had she not been able to change—to support her children's decision to follow Jesus and be available to the moment. The Lord of Glory would have passed her by and gone to the home of a neighbor. Next time we are caught in the middle of a very hard and unusual day, perhaps we could ask, "Is Jesus in this somewhere?" It isn't always peaceful at the center of his will.

The Household Miracle: Mark 1:29–34

Did you catch the bit about the iron knife and hair braid? Healers in first century Israel did not know about germs and viruses and contagion. There were no miracle drugs. Medicine was filled with a good bit of magic and *mumbo jumbo*. The prescribed Jewish cure for the "burning fever" was to tie an iron knife to a thorn bush by a hair braid and chant a selected scripture. Really! Several reliable historians describe it. No doubt Peter's family tried that cure immediately when the fever came on, but, as usual, it was not working. Nothing to do but wait the fever out in misery, drink some herbal tea, and pray that it would abate.

Jesus arrived and skipped all the protocol, took her hand and helped her up, and she was healed. Luke's version says he spoke a rebuke to the fever as he did this (Luke 4:39). In fact, she was healed so thoroughly that she got up and helped serve them at dinner!

No braids, no knives, no bushes! Just a touch and a word. No wonder the townspeople could barely wait out the Sabbath before bringing him throngs of sick folks to heal. Jesus was an immediate celebrity, and the household of Peter and Andrew provided the stage. Very likely at this point, if there had been any skepticism on the part of Peter's mother-in-law, along with Salome and Zebedee and others of the parent generation, it was swept away in gratitude and faith. It would have made giving a son or son-in-law to the gospel ministry a much more joyful sacrifice, knowing that this Jesus was exactly who he claimed to be. There may have even been a touch of parental pride in having a child be part of a movement headed by so notable a prophet. "Yes, my son-in-law is one of the chosen Disciples of Jesus of Nazareth—the Healer, you know. They are very close."

Touch Point

Jesus' ministry was many things, but most of all it was always person-centered. In the privacy of a little home in Capernaum he

did a miracle for one middle-aged lady with a need. He cared. He cared for her then, and he cares for each one of us today.

Jesus does not have to have big crowds to reach out with power. He does not favor the lovely or cater to the top of the social ladder. He is not impressed with shows of piety or lengthy prayers. He does not call in the media or blow a horn before his deeds. If there is a need—even a very private need—and he is asked to help, he is there. Trust him in this.

On Their Way: Mark 1:35–39

People handle celebrity in different ways. It is heady stuff, and even Jesus had to sort things out from time to time. We can see here his secret: a powerful prayer life. His decisions were not based on how people responded, on his rating in the morning paper, on the success of numbers. He kept his focus by "calling home." Early, before the day began, he got up and prayed for direction. And his Father in the "real world" clarified for him the strategy of the Kingdom. So he moved on. It's a reliable formula for finding the will of God today also, be we famous or just common worker folks: *Keep an ear to heaven and two feet on the ground!*

Wonderful as the miracles of healing were for that community, this was not the primary thing Jesus came to do. "Let us go…to nearby villages—so I can preach there also." The message of the gospel was his program. Compassionate healings were simply a picture of his heart.

That morning the small band of followers packed their bags and began the long trek around Galilee, town to town, synagogue to synagogue, sometimes by foot, sometimes by borrowed fishing boat. In every town desperate people pled for physical healing; it was freely given. And as Jesus dispensed cures, he also told the Good News: "You can become a child of God."

I think "Esther" was proud to have her son-in-law be a part of that.

Chapter 6

Desperate and Delivered

Three Mothers of Sick Children
Jairus' Wife (Luke 8:40–56)
Widow of Nain (Luke 7:11–17)
Canaanite Woman (Mark 7:24–30)

Tabitha looked curiously at the four strangers talking with her parents. The past few hours were a blank spot in her memory. "What happened, Mama?" she whispered. "Why are these men here?" But her mother shook off the question guardedly, and she knew to wait.

After her father escorted the visitors beyond the tapestry door, Tabitha asked again. "Mama? What happened to me? Why did those strangers come?"

Leah fell on her daughter's neck and smothered her with kisses of relief. "Oh, my baby, my baby," she sobbed. "God has given you back to us. Praise his name! Praise his name!"

Tabitha hugged her mother, but quickly wiggled free. "Mama! Mama, I'm all right! Don't cry—just tell me what happened. I must have slept all the way through it."

A servant came in with a bowl of warm porridge and two loaves of bread. "So good to see you well, Miss Tabitha," she said, and then disappeared the way she had come before Tabitha could answer.

"Eat, Dear," Leah told her. "You haven't had nourishment in several days. And you are so thin. Just look at you!" Leah ran her hands along her daughter's thin arm and ribs as she spoke, but Tabitha was too busy gulping down the porridge to protest.

Something outside the window caught the girl's eye, and she jumped up in time to see a sight more compelling than her hunger. "There goes Granny Lois and the mourners, Mama. Look! Flutes and all. Who died?"

Leah searched for words, wondering how much to tell her twelve-year-old about the last two days' happenings. "I guess you did, Darling," she answered quietly.

"I did?" Tabitha was confused. "I thought I was just asleep, Mama." She thought about it for a few more bites. "Was I really *dead?*"

"I think so, child. Yes, you were dead," Leah admitted. "And the rabbi, Jesus of Nazareth, came and wakened you from death, and gave you back to us. O, praise God!" Once more she hugged her child with mighty relief.

Tabitha tore a generous chunk from her bread and dipped it into the porridge. "Mama…." Her mouth was so full she could barely speak. "Look! You have your new dress on backwards…and it is torn…a really big tear. It's ruined! How come?"

Leah fingered the rend over her shoulder. "It was for…I guess I tore it when they told me you were dead, Tabitha. Don't fret—I can fix it…later."

Judah, the *unpedigreed* family pup, pushed uninvited through the tapestry doorway and jumped up on Tabitha's leg. Reaching down to scratch his ears, Tabitha pursued the conversation. "And Daddy? What did Daddy do when they said I was dead?"

"He had gone to find Jesus and beg him to come and heal you. He wasn't here," Leah explained. "They got here a while later. Something happened along the way, and they were delayed."

Tabitha lay back on her favorite big cushion, trying to take in all the wonders. Judah crawled into her lap, sniffing the empty bowl in vain hope of a handout. She gave him the last chunk of bread, and he happily set about licking the broth from her fingers. Judah loved lamb and all things that smelled like it. "Isn't that Jesus the one who healed the possessed man on the Sabbath day in Daddy's synagogue and upset the rulers and Pharisees so?"

Leah was folding the bedding that had covered her daughter's pallet. She didn't look up. "Yes, Tabitha. He is the one."

"So why did Daddy call for him? It will make the others angry with us, won't it?" she persisted.

Leah turned toward this little girl who was growing up so fast before her eyes. "We were absolutely desperate, Darling," she answered. "You were dying, and we had done everything we could do. None of the cures was working, and the healers had given you up for dead. Jesus was the only one we knew of who might help. We had to try him."

Both fell silent. Tabitha reached up to hug her mother, and Leah dropped to the mat to gather her precious daughter to her arms.

"I'm sorry I scared you so badly, Mama, but I'm glad I didn't die yet," the girl said softly.

Leah could only hold her child close and cry.

Behind the Scene
A Study of Luke 8:40–56, Luke 7:11–17, and Mark 7:24–30

Three Mothers: Alike and Different

There is no desperation like the desperation of a parent with an incurable child. That is the common thread in these three stories. The widowed mother of Nain had just watched her only child—a son—die, and was on the way to bury him in the cemetery east of town, when Jesus happened upon them and raised her son to life. The Canaanite woman from the area of Tyre had a daughter possessed of a demonic illness. She heard that the Jews had a powerful rabbi who was visiting the area and intruded on his privacy with an urgent request for her daughter's healing. And Jairus' wife (we have named her "Leah"), watching her lovely young daughter waste away, urged her husband to cross the strong taboos of the Pharisees and beg Jesus for help. All were desperate, and all were delivered. Three happier endings we could never have written.

The curiosity is this: none of these mothers actually knew Jesus or believed in him as their own Messiah and Lord. At least, not until *after* they experienced his power in their personal family tragedies. So if faith were a requirement for Jesus' help, none of these women would qualify. The widow of Nain did not even know Jesus was near. She never saw him through her tears, or asked for his help. Jesus just walked up, stopped the funeral procession, and healed the boy! The Canaanite woman was not even a Jew. She was not looking for a Messiah for herself. She happened to hear about Jesus' great powers and asked to borrow him for a minute to fix a desperate situation in her Gentile family. And Jairus—and probably "Leah"—were part of the Jewish establishment that had rejected Jesus as a radical and a fake—until all the prescribed cures and prayers failed them and they had to swallow their pride and beg for his help.

First, the Widow of Nain: Luke 7:11–17

Jesus raised three people from the dead in his short but miraculous ministry. The first was this boy at Nain. It was not that Jesus hadn't healed plenty of folks already; he just had not resuscitated anyone before, so the miracle was a big surprise to his many followers. Isn't that one of the wonderful things about following Jesus—finding that he is be able to do so much more than we thought he could? Paul described it when he said, "Now unto him who is able to do immeasurably more than all we ask or imagine, according to his power that is at work within us…" (Ephesians 3:20).

The second wonderful thing here is discovering Jesus' incredible compassion. The grieving mother did not even ask for his help. She had been swept through the most awful hours of her life, watching helplessly as her only child, her "only begotten son," moved through the throes of whatever took his life. At his death, kinfolk and neighbors would have taken hold where she could not and called for professional mourners to come and express her grief. They would have washed his body, cut his hair, and anointed him with perfumed oil. He would have been wrapped in linen and placed in an open wicker hammock for the procession to the "field of weepers." While his mother could only cry, they would have helped her rend and reverse her garments, and then set her behind the bier for the sad trek eastward. While she was too overcome for words, they would have chanted good things about his life as they walked. The whole village had turned out to console her, as small towns often do for one of their own.

Jesus heard their loud obituary, called above the mournful flutes. "He was a good and kind son, the only son of his mother, who cared for her tenderly. Now he has been taken away, and she is left alone with nobody to care for her in her old age." It was customary for everyone to step aside in respectful silence as the procession passed. Jesus and the large crowd with him likely did exactly that. But it did not satisfy his tender heart. Stepping forward, he stopped the procession—itself an improper thing to do—and touched the bier. This was an unheard-of act, one that rendered him unclean for worship. He then spoke to the corpse, saying: "Young man, get up!"

Why did he do that? Why does he ever intervene for us in our desperate times? His heart is touched when we are caught in the traumas of our lives. Sometimes, like this mother, we are so deep into our grief we do not even realize he is there. Sometimes we forget even to ask for his help. But he is watching. He knows. He cares. He weeps with us at our gravesites.

Before anyone could exhale, the dead son sat up in his hammock and began to talk. And now we see a third wonderful thing about Jesus in this story. His miracle caused the people to praise and believe in God, and that is the whole reason Jesus had come to Nain—to bring people to the realization of God. "For I have come down from heaven not to do my will but to do the will of him who sent me." "I have brought you glory on earth by completing the work you gave me to do." (John 6:38, 17:4)

It was springtime in Galilee. As pallbearers helped the young man out of the hammock, his mother ran to hug his neck, and the two of them, mobbed by amazed family and well-wishers, walked through fields of wild-flowers towards home. New life had come to Nain that lovely day!

Touch Point

Reflect one more time on the three wonderful findings of this story:

1. **Jesus is able to do more than we often expect him to do.**
2. **Jesus is a person of incredible compassion.**
3. **Jesus does what brings praise and glory to God.**

In our most desperate times Jesus intervenes; sometimes because we ask, and sometimes because of his great compassion and love. In all this, we are so blessed to have a Savior who cares.

Second, Jairus' Wife: Luke 8:40–56.

Of these three stories, this is probably most familiar, because it is in all three of the Synoptic Gospels (see also Matthew 9:18–26 and Mark 5:21–43). Jesus and his band were returning by boat to their Capernaum home base after having a series of harrowing experiences on the east side of the lake. First had come the great storm, which nearly swamped them. Jesus stilled it with a good scolding. Then the terrifying encounter with the maniacal man who lived in the cave tombs of Gadara happened. In retaliation for the loss of their demon-possessed swine herd, which jumped off the cliff in madness, the Gadarenes ran the *Jesus Team* out of town.

Now home at last, there was still more trauma in the air. Out of the anxious, noisy, welcoming crowd came the synagogue official, Jairus. Everyone knew him—no surprise there. The unexpected thing was how he threw himself at Jesus' feet in humility and desperation and pled for help. After all, hadn't the Pharisees and rulers been furious shortly before this, when Jesus healed a possessed man in the Sabbath service? (See Luke 4:33–35.) And when he disregarded the Sabbath rule in order to glean grain and heal a crippled man? (See Luke 6:1–11.)

Back at Jairus' house, the mother had stayed by her dying daughter's bed, trying every cure known, praying every prayer, hoping every hope. We aren't told her name, or her daughter's. ("Leah" and "Tabitha" just sounded like they fit these two.) Nor are we told what illness was taking her child's life. We might guess that it was a recurring malaria, a persistent typhus, or a common dysentery. All of these were frequent in the area. Whatever the rabbis had suggested, we can be certain this mother had tried. Picture the girl wearing amulets of family charms around her neck, plastered with a poultice of lard and herbs, swathed in damp rags to cool her fever. Such were common cures of the day.

Have you known up close a parent with an incurable child? Modern medicine has come far, and most visits to physicians result in cures. But still the dreaded words can come: "We just don't have a cure for this yet." "This may work, or it may not. But we'll keep trying, and eventually one of the medications may be effective." "We'll do our best, but the numbers on this disease are not very encouraging." "I'm afraid this will be very lengthy and expensive, and the insurance may not agree to pay." "This is in God's Hands now. If you believe in prayer, now is the time. There is really little more we can do besides keep her comfortable." Even with words like those, few mothers give up. They will pray, hope, rock, sing, encourage, cry—but they will hang in there, even until death. Mothers are just that way.

The difference for Christians is that we have a Savior who answers prayer, and prayer is real! It may be weak and inadequate, as was the faith of Jairus. It may be a last resort, as his probably was. At our very best, we are never powerful enough to effect a cure through our prayers alone. With the father in Mark 9:24 we cry, "Lord, I do believe; help me overcome my unbelief!" Then we wait for Jesus' assurance in our souls, knowing, "Everything is possible to him who believes" (vs. 23). Jesus wants to heal us, he always can, and he usually does. And that is why prayer is very effective for us in our crises today.

The interesting thing is that Jairus' and Leah's prayer received a delayed response (note the intervening story in Luke 8:42–48). Why would Jesus dally on the way to answering a request as desperate as this? Why are prayers not often answered with the lightning speed we think they deserve? The earthly response time of Jesus to Jairus is not a good comparison to our own situations today. We know that in Jesus' heavenly position he is not limited by place and distance—and we are not subject to "standing in line for our turn," as Jairus was. A valid parallel with Jairus, however, is the way Jesus' answer is not tied to *our* timeframes. He could have healed

"Tabitha" *before* her death—or after. He knew that, and so told the frantic father: "Don't be afraid; only believe, and she will be healed." We tend to impose upon Jesus our limitations, expecting him to respond as a human would. He is above and beyond all that, and his answers are—well—his answers, not our small solutions.

It happened in the third instance of raising the dead also. Remember Lazarus? That time, Jesus actually delayed his coming deliberately, the Scripture says, so that the power of God would be more spectacular and unmistakable. "This sickness will not end in death. No, it is for God's glory, so that God's Son may be glorified through it" (John 11:4). Perhaps another value of these stories becomes clear as we learn to look for ways to glorify and magnify God in our darkest times. We must learn to trust him with our crises. We must learn to trust him with our children. He loves them more than we ever could.

The question creeps in, *Were they really dead, these three: the widow's son, Jairus' little girl, and Lazarus?* Many excellent Bible interpreters believe they could have been in a deathlike coma or trance, deeper than the primitive methods of the first century could diagnose. The rest of that theory is that Jesus came in each time and wakened the comatose person, and then he/she was pronounced "healed." How likely is it that a person so near death's door would so immediately be up talking, walking, and eating? Recovery in such severe illness usually takes days—even weeks. It all comes down to believing that Jesus was God's Son. If we can come that far, the doubts then dissolve in our faith.

Touch Point

Have you had difficult experiences in prayer? Perhaps you have struggled with an incurable disease, a birth defect, an untimely death or other crisis, and wondered why your prayers were not answered in the way you asked. Someone may have told you there are certain formulas or "tricks" to getting prayers answered. Not so. God does not play games with us. One of the best lessons of these stories is that Jesus is a friend, not a reluctant adversary. There are no secret codes, no gimmicks to employ with him. Promises are promises, and God keeps his as they apply to our best interest.

Each time Jesus raised a person from death he gave them additional time. At a later point, each of them died again. We pray for that good time, that brief reprieve for the ones we love, because we cannot imagine anything better than life on earth. Often through medical miracles, or just by his grace, God answers that prayer on this side of the divide, where we can see and be part of it. At other times, he answers it beyond our horizon, raising the person to life again in his Presence, in heavenly realms. Either way, our prayers are answered. We have to trust God's judgment on the "where" of it. As my wise, twelve-year-old friend recently told me, "Sometimes people have to die to get well."

Finally, the Canaanite Woman: Mark 7:24–30

Jesus was looking for a place to take his men for seclusion and study. The border of Upper Galilee and Phoenicia offered some remote places, so there it would be. No doubt all of them looked forward to leaving the crowds and the opposition behind. But anonymity escaped them, and their location became known to the residents of the district.

Somewhere in the area, a Gentile mother with a difficult burden to bear was desperate for help. Her small child was possessed of a wicked disease that disrupted the family day and night. The mother was at wit's end, and when she heard the Jewish man with power to heal was within walking distance, she left her family in someone's care and set out for help.

What about his demon thing, we might ask? First century people believed in demons by the legions. To them, they were everywhere—under rocks and in trees, hiding in graveyards, and inhabiting the air on every hand. Today we don't think that way, so how are we to approach a story like this one? The safest way is to do as Jesus did. He responded to people on their level of readiness. If there were demons, he respected those demons. If it was superstition and ignorance, he still met them on the ground where they stood. She claimed demons, and he healed demons. The result was a healed daughter, and that is what all schools of thought can celebrate.

But what of Jesus' unusual answer to her request? The conversation went something like this.

The woman, by Matthew's account (15:23) had been crying out to the Disciples for a while before she got past them and burst uninvited into Jesus' privacy. When she blurted out her request, Jesus took a deep breath and did not answer. The Disciples, ever ready to protect and assist, filled his silence by suggesting that she be bounced back out the door—well, not physically, of course; but she was, after all, an unclean Gentile "dog." Little respect was due her.

Jesus' answer is so *un-Jesus-like* to our senses. "I was sent only to the children of Israel. I can't take the food meant for the family and give it to their dogs," he explained.

Thirteen big men were not enough to discourage this mother. After all, she had been doing battle with demons every day for many years. "But the dogs get to eat the crumbs the children toss them under the table," she insisted. Who could resist her request, made with such humility and perseverance? Who could deny her in the face of such desperate hope? Surely not Jesus, who loved children. So he gave her what she asked for, and they all got back to the business at hand. If even a Gentile, a woman, an impertinent mother, could ask of Jesus and receive an answer to her need, how much more can we?

Touch Point

Some think this story may have been the basis of Jesus' later parable, told in Luke 18:1–8, about the persistent widow. Both stories give us an important insight about God. He respects and listens when we feel strongly enough about something to bring it before him continuously over time. Does he grant unwise requests? Never that. But he does reward persistent faith. A good thing to remember when a problem that plagues us just will not go away.

How ever many times you have prayed about it, pray again. God will either reward the prayer or show you a better way to pray. Romans 8:26–27 contains a wonderful assurance regarding times when we are too burdened, or too exhausted, or too desperate to know how to approach God with our needs. At those times we can rest in him, knowing his Spirit within will speak to the Father for us. Prayer isn't such a hard thing to do. For God's child, it is simply coming into his Presence, knowing that he *will* be there, he will *listen,* and he will *care.*

Chapter 7

Fragile Faith

The Woman Who Anointed Him
(Luke 7:36–50)

Judith pressed closer into the crowd, hoping to hear better and see more, yet cautious not to jostle those around her. *Where did all these people come from? How did they know of this rabbi?* she wondered. Some she recognized as neighbors from the Capernaum area but others, judging by their travel bags and weary eyes, had come many miles. It was all the talk at work today—this Rabbi Jesus who had been visiting the synagogues nearby, healing unbelievable diseases—even freeing people from demons.

The morning and midday had been spent helping Simon's wife prepare tonight's company meal, and Judith was happy for the work. This very rabbi would be the honored guest. But, not being needed to serve, she would not be attending the occasion. Now she was making her way home when the gathered crowd caught her attention. Out of curiosity she stopped to listen a minute.

Just in front of her a mother, holding a sleeping child, grew too weary to stand any longer and cautiously shoved her way out. Judith quickly stepped forward. At the same moment, the woman to her left lurched for the same space. "Oh, excuse me," Judith apologized.

The startled woman looked up, but when she saw who had touched her a scowl shadowed her face. Pulling her shawl tightly about her shoulders to make herself smaller, she whispered to a companion, "I should think the sinners would have stayed home." The two nodded in pompous agreement. Judith flushed, but stood her ground. She had grown to expect slurs from the righteous and self-righteous of her world. Long since she had accepted that she'd made her choices—not very good ones—and she would now have to live with them.

The rabbi was still speaking as Judith's mind focused back on the scene. He seemed unusually authoritative, yet not scathing, as rabbis often were. He had "come to seek and save the lost," he said, and then launched into a story about a man whose son left home to gain freedom but wound up wasting his life. Judith could feel her broken spirit resonate with the tale. The son had stayed gone a long time, squandered his inheritance, and broken his father's heart. Still, the father loved him and had not given up hope of his return.

Judith's hand went to the necklace vial on her chest. She grasped it tightly and pressed it to her lips as the rabbi spoke. It was the last gift from her broken-hearted mother to the wayward daughter she thought she had lost forever. The memory of the scene was still fresh in her mind. Judith was just over twelve years old when her father promised her as a bride to Caleb, the fish merchant's son. Judith had hated Caleb since he caught her alone on the goatpath when they were children and forced his passions on her with brute strength. Her father never knew it. She was certain he would have punished her severely for allowing it to happen. And Caleb was too clever to let his coarse desire for her show. So the deal was made.

Had she stayed there, the marriage would have been without escape. But a month before the wedding, while out tending the flock one drizzly, dreary afternoon, Judith left her home and set out for Magdala, hoping for a better life and maybe a job in the dye works. Her father managed to round up the abandoned flock—most of it, anyway. But he was left with a broken marriage contract to fulfill and the embarrassment of a divorced and runaway daughter. His rage never abated, and she soon learned from trusted friends that she had been disinherited from her family.

Magdala turned out to be the first of her bad choices. With just fourteen short years of experience, Judith had no idea how hard it could be to break into a new town and a new life. Lacking a better plan, she stopped by an inn and asked for a few nights' room and board in exchange for her labors. Her small frame was hard-pressed to keep up with the innkeep's stout wife and daughters as they rushed from chore to chore, from daylight to dark.

She made a friend in Dinah, the daughter just younger than she. But the older son, Levi, was a nuisance at the beginning—and later something of a threat.

At first it was a game—his meeting her at every turn when nobody was looking. But after a severe scolding from the innkeeper and with her livelihood dependent on her work, she found his attentions menacing. Eventually he caught her and violated her. "No one will have you now if you tell," he jeered in contempt. "But I'll let you stay here—as long as you please me." Judith was aching to go home, but by now there was no home to go back to.

It was almost ten years and two children later that she had gathered up her tattered courage and returned to Capernaum, broken and ashamed. Unable to go to her parents' home, she found an abandoned place on the edge of town and ran out the rats, scorpions, and doves that had taken it over. With great effort she salvaged a few pots and a broken table from the remains, and made the one room livable for herself and her sons. Here and there Judith found work and kept them all alive. But starting over was hard, and she was determined not to beg. Widows were cared for—divorcees were shunned. The only easy money came at a terrible price, and there are few secrets in a small town.

Looking carefully for a time when her father would be away fishing, Judith managed a tearful reunion with her mother and was shocked to find her very ill and nearly bedfast. True to her mother's heart, she found some old sleeping mats and linens that Judith and the boys could use until they could get better things. She even gave them a nanny goat for milk. As Judith left, her mother pressed into her hand her only real treasure—the vial of rose oil she had worn around her neck for years. Judith managed a smile and held her tears back for the short walk to her shack.

The rabbi's story ended happily, as Judith would have liked for hers to end. As the wayward son returned, dirty and broken, his father ran out to meet him and forgave him. It was the story of a second chance, and love that would not die. *"Come home! Whatever you have done, the Father still loves you,"* was the message that seemed too good to be true. For her it had not been true. How Judith hurt for such a reunion with her own father, but knew it was outside of possibility.

The rabbi was still teaching as Judith slipped away from the crowd and continued toward home, bone-weary and deeply saddened. Reaching the house she set about fixing something for the boys to eat when they returned from school. With the lamp flame she rekindled the hearth fire, then set a pot of leftover lentils on to warm. Turning about, she went for the flour and oil to make bread. Supplies were low and "Mammy" would be dry another two weeks. Then the boys could share her milk with her hungry new kid. A few early figs were ripe, and that, with the lentils and flatbread, would be the evening meal. She hoped the boys did not know how desperately poor they really were. *If I had made better choices, my sons would have had a better life,* she thought. The reality brought fresh pain. Fiercely Judith fought back tears. *Too late to cry now. All we can do is go on—there is just no other way out.*

Waiting for the children, she scratched in the garden a little. The rains were late. When the boys came home she would have to send them to the spring for water or the tender onions and melons would not survive long. The grapes were setting on well. Judith was grateful for whatever former tenant had put vines and fruit trees into the yard. At times they made the difference between putting two boys to bed hungry or fed.

The old olive tree stump invited her to rest. *"Come home! Whatever you have done, the Father still loves you,"* echoed in her mind. The rabbi's message kept floating back to her thoughts. How she wished it could be so! How she longed to hear more from this one who was looking for lost ones to rescue. *If anyone needs rescuing, surely it is me,* she thought. The idea came suddenly: *Suppose I were to join the gallery at the dinner tonight and listen as the rabbi teaches? What could it hurt? Many people will come, and if I stay in the shadows, nobody will know I am there. If ever my life is to change, I must find a way to get back into the blessings of God. I hope and pray that this Jesus Rabbi, can show me the way.*

Behind the Scene
A Study of Luke 7:36–50 and 8:1–3

Finding a Way to God: Luke 7:36–38

Did you read the whole story in Scripture? Seldom has the picture been so clear—the steps that take us back into God's grace. "Judith" (our name for this nameless, repentant woman) shows them to us.

First is her sense of need. She was well-aware of her sin and willing to admit that she had gone astray. Her pain was obvious. It took great courage for her to step forward among the people who condemned her daily. Yet something compelled her to come to Jesus. She was a sinner, and she needed him! There was a great emptiness—a great despair—in her soul.

Second is her understanding that forgiveness is available for the lost. We have no idea when or where she came to hear Jesus' message, but apparently, somewhere on the Capernaum shore or nearby hills, she listened to his teaching. It is even possible that she heard it secondhand from a friend who had heard and believed. Many in Capernaum and Galilee were catching on. Whatever, she had somehow come to realize that *God alone* offers the forgiveness, cleansing, and peace she so desperately lacked. She knew that what Jesus taught was exactly the answer for her.

Next is her repentant spirit. The tears did not save her, but they signaled that something was happening in her heart. She came to Jesus because she wanted to be forgiven and to change her lifestyle. She was ready to experience grace. Sad is the person who acknowledges need and understands grace, yet turns away. This brave lady followed through, stumbling past the jeers and slurs of the *religious types* who looked on.

Fourth is her belief in Jesus. She chose not to go to the synagogue, to be cleansed by keeping The Law. Or to Simon, the Pharisee host, a man of arrogance and scorn. She certainly knew she could not rescue herself —that effort had been doomed from the start. She saw forgiveness only in Jesus and went straight to him for her salvation. "Your faith has saved you," he said. Her faith—however fragile—was very real to Jesus.

Lastly, she confessed her faith openly. It is never easy to admit sin and ask forgiveness before others, but a woman with a past opens herself to great condemnation by doing so. She did not feel valued by the crowd of onlookers at that supper. Although she desperately needed and wanted their acceptance, she had no expectation of being offered a loving "hand of fellowship" when her decision was made public. Still, she stepped out into the crowded room and declared her faith by a sweet sacrifice to her new Lord. And the perfume of her faith was shared by all.

And she was "forgiven much." There is no life so bad, no sin so great, that Jesus' sacrifice cannot cover it. From the mouth of the Lord Jesus himself came the words: "Your sins are forgiven... Your faith has saved you. Go in peace." (Skip to verses 48 and 50.)

It is a path that is open to every woman—every person. And we believe it is the *only* path. "I am the way and the truth and the life. *No one comes to the father except through me*" (John 14:6).

Touch Point

This may be the most important opportunity for reflection in this book. Look back over the pathway to God illustrated by our

lady and walk it with her. Have you been there also?

1. Have you admitted your own need for salvation?
2. Understood that God provides forgiveness through Jesus?
3. Repented of your past?
4. Believed in Jesus fully and only for salvation?
5. Confessed your faith openly before others?

Wonderful forgiveness and peace come when Christ is made Savior and Lord. You can do it right here, right now, if you will.

A Contrast of Spirits: Luke 7:39–47

Here we can see it: an arrogant host, a broken woman, and a compassionate Savior. Jesus knew Simon was miles from understanding God's unconditional grace toward this fallen woman, so he told him a story. And now we are treated to a story within a story.

In choosing a story to expose the attitudes of Simon, his Pharisee host, Jesus met him on his own turf. He talked about money. Simon had it all. He was a community leader, respected, a man with authority. He had passed all the tests of religion with flying colors. He had a lovely home and family. By contrast, this lady had little or nothing. The vial of perfume may have been her only valuable possession.

Correction: Simon had all but *good manners.* Why had he bothered to invite Jesus as a special guest if he planned to treat him shabbily? All the amenities given a visiting rabbi were missing. No water for his dusty feet. No kiss of welcome. No perfumed oil for his hair. It was left to the sinful, unlettered woman to provide all of those things. Simon does not come off as a sincere follower, or even a seeker. Instead he shows himself to be a skeptic. *"If* this man were a prophet, which I was certain he *wasn't* before I invited him…," seems to be the flavor of things. Perhaps he invited Jesus out of curiosity, or in hopes of tricking him and discrediting him. Perhaps it seemed the politically correct thing to do. Maybe this was just entertainment for his guests.

Second correction: Simon had all but good manners *and compassion.* Simon would not touch a prostitute, but Jesus let her touch him, caress him, kiss him. Simon could see no value in her, but Jesus saw her as one to die for. Simon could only see her reputation, but Jesus saw her heart and honored her faith. The sad truth is that the synagogue, the religious leaders, and the community could have reached out to help this broken woman come back to God. But apparently no one cared enough to find a way—until Jesus came to town.

Touch Point

Simon the Pharisee illustrates clearly for us the difference between being religious and being Christlike. It is sadly possible to be religious and still be intolerant, arrogant, and

**skeptical. The infamous Proverbs 6:16–19
passage, "Six things the Lord hates…" begins
with pride, or arrogance.**

**Maybe the way we see and value people
is the truest of all tests of our love for Jesus.
In I John 2:9–11 we are warned about saying
we love the Lord while treating our brother
(sister) badly. Judging people by outward
appearance, financial means, or reputation
is a habit we must lose, because this mindset
works contrary to the attributes of Christ,
whose likeness the Spirit is ever-striving to
create in us (see Galatians 5:22–26).**

"Go in Peace": Luke 7:48–50 (and 8:1–3)

We would love to have been there for this last in-
terchange (7:48–50). Did Jesus smile at her as he sent
her "into peace"? Did she thank him quietly…or simply
nod and disappear in joyful silence? Jewish men did
not generally have permission to speak to a woman in
public, so the scene may have been more reserved than
Hollywood would picture it.

What new life waited for this forgiven woman as she
left the party that night? Sense tells us all her problems
were waiting for her when she got home. Attitudes do not
change just because someone makes a decision to receive
Christ as Savior and Lord. Did the synagogue accept her
with open arms? Did her family believe her and give her
another chance? Did anyone step forward to give her a
hug and a smile? Did she find her way somehow?

Jesus shortly took off on another mission trip, with his Disciples (8:1–3). And, lo!—he took some women along this time! Notice who they were: "…some women who had been cured of evil spirits and diseases." Since 500 A.D. church people have conjectured that our forgiven lady was one of these. Some think she was Mary Magdalene, although there is no proof (and some reasonable doubt) that it could have been she. "Judith" would surely have found safe company among others who had experienced a dark past and the healing miracle of Jesus' grace, as she had.

What matters is this: *there is life after brokenness!* Jesus called into his service women who had come to him in desperate need. He healed them and gave them a new purpose for living—that of ministering to (and with) him and his men as they went on a mission. Whatever their past, whatever reputation had shadowed them until now, Jesus treated them as what they were: whole and worthy persons. And in taking them away from their former residences (probably on an occasional, intermittent schedule) they had a fresh audience with whom to share their stories.

Look at who they were. Always mentioned first is Mary of Magdala, "from whom seven devils had come out." She followed Jesus all over Galilee, to Jerusalem, to the Cross, to the grave, and very likely to Pentecost. She is in every Gospel account of the Crucifixion and the Resurrection. (See Luke 23:55, 24:10; John 19:25, 20:1; Mark 15:40–41; Matthew 27:55–56, 28:1; and Acts 1:14). We will meet her again, and more intimately, in later chapters of this book.

With her is a lady of the court whose husband was Herod's financial manager. Her name is Joanna, and she, too, followed Jesus to the Cross. (Some think she is the wife of the nobleman whose story is told in John 4:46–54, but that is an educated guess, at best—and more likely a stretch.) Next Susanna—never mentioned before or after this time—but possibly among the "many others" noted elsewhere in lists of women. (If I were to choose, I would pick Susanna as our "Judith" in the story above). These are the *healed ones* who are identified to us. It is an interesting blending of backgrounds and personalities of those now, "accepted in the Beloved."

Along with them (in the accounts referred to above) are several mothers of the Disciples. They include Mary, who was the mother of James, the younger, and Joses, and probably also the wife of Clopas (maybe Cleopas?) Also Salome, the mother of James and John, who may also have been the sister of Jesus' mother; and Mary, the mother of Jesus. Check out the references. Make a chart. You will have joy thinking about this first Women's Missionary Action Group!

Touch Point

One unnamed prostitute with a small vial of rose oil around her neck has cast a fragrance that leaves for us the essence of faith, showing us how to come to God and how to live for him afterwards. Next time you pass a hooker, look with new eyes. Jesus may have claimed her as his own.

Chapter 8

One Touch

The Woman Sick Twelve Years
(Mark 5:21–34)

The house was still dark when Abigail wakened to the sound of cooing doves in the pomegranate tree outside her window. For a few minutes she lay listening, as the near one called and the far one answered in almost identical tones. It was hard to get up in the springtime morning chill. After a night's rest she still felt as tired as she had the night before.

Rolling up her mat quietly, she set it into the far corner behind the chest, where Eli and Jacob would not accidentally touch it. Then she began her morning routine of bathing and changing her undergarments. The issue had been especially bothersome of late, and Abigail had limited her time away from the house because of it.

Ready now to meet the day, she tiptoed out her doorway to the cooking yard, so as not to waken her husband and youngest son. They had returned just yesterday evening from two Sabbaths in the fields with the sheep and needed all the sleep they could get. Sheep-herding took the men away so much at this time of year. Eli was very particular about his flocks. He knew every sheep by name—even the new lambs born just a month or two prior. Everything both families had was invested in the flocks, and Eli guarded them well.

He and Jacob would be home only two nights, so she had washing and cooking to do to prepare for their return. Eli left the sheep only when supplies were low and when he could leave them in the care of his older sons. James and Joseph knew shepherding from beginning to end. They had been raised up with the ewes, but there were always new dangers in the hills. Eli would not leave them alone for long. It was at these times that they all felt keenly the loss of his brother, Jude, who had died from the fever the previous winter. For many years they'd combined flocks and shared the care of the animals. Now Eli had just the boys and himself, and both flocks to tend.

Abigail stirred up the cooking coals and had a pot of water heating for porridge when the sun finally inched its way over the roof of the synagogue and filtered through the date palm. It was nippy, and her shawl felt good. She tucked the ends of it into her dress to keep them from catching in the cooking flames as she stirred the gruel. A gentle nudge from behind told her Freckles was ready to be milked. "Silly goat," she whispered, as she reached for an empty pot to catch the spurts. Eli liked his milk warm and fresh.

A cloth covered yesterday's food, and Abigail flipped back a corner to remind herself what was left. There were plenty of figs, some goat cheese, and a few dried fishes. She would send Jacob to pick a couple of oranges when he wakened. As the porridge thickened she mixed a little goat milk, oil, and meal, and shaped flat loaves to bake on the hearthstones. The chores were familiar and mindless, but she loved caring for her family. She just wished she felt stronger.

Setting the food to the side where they could easily find it, she again covered it with a cloth. Then she turned toward the house to gather soiled garments for the wash. Shepherding is a rough and dirty job, and there were always clothes to wash and mend. She was startled to see Eli standing in the doorway, watching her silently. "Shalom. What's for my breakfast?" he smiled.

"It's all ready, there by the fire," she said, indicating the food with a nod of her head. His strong frame made her feel safe. She yearned for the days when she could reach around his chest and hug him hard, but while this issue lasted she was not permitted to do so. The separation left a longing neither could deal with very well. Eli stepped aside as she grabbed the soap and a basket and went in to get the wash. "I'll be back soon," she called, and left by the other door, barely stopping to kiss the parchment on the way.

It was not a long walk to the washing pool at the creek. Abigail wanted to get there early, then get away before the other women came. Some folks didn't like to share the creek with a sick person. It was so hard always to be thought of as *unclean*. The day promised to be sunny, which was good. The clothes would dry quickly.

She was on her last two garments when Adah came, bringing a big bundle of wash for her large family. "Hi, sis! Thought I'd catch you here," she greeted, bending to hug her sister.

"You're not supposed to touch me, you know," Abigail teased. "I'm unclean."

"That's for the men folks, Abbie," Adah countered. "I'll hug you whenever I wish. They can't write a law against sisters hugging." And she gave her sister one more defiant squeeze. "Are you feeling any better? Did that last cure help any?"

"No." Abigail's answer was short and terse. "I almost knew it wouldn't help before I tried it, but after twelve years of bleeding I'm so tired of being sick and left out, I was ready to try anything."

"Even an ostrich egg's ashes in a linen rag?" Adah giggled.

"Or ass's dung with barley corns," Abigail shot back. "Anything! I just want to be well."

"I know you must be very discouraged," Adah sympathized.

"*Very!*" Tears welled up and her chin trembled, but Abigail tried not to cry. "Eli is a patient man, but we've had no real closeness since Jacob was born eleven years ago. Almost twelve, in fact. We have a good life, but—we just can't sleep together or eat together. That's very hard on a marriage. I can't even hug my sons without breaking

The Law." Persistent tears ran down to the wash water as she pounded the last garment furiously on the stone. "It's not my fault, Addie! It's not my fault! I just wish someone could do something for me."

Adah watched her younger sister sadly. "You're gonna beat that shirt to shreds, sis." Both of them giggled through tears. "They just can't get inside a woman's body to fix it." Adah made a part in the middle of her sister's tousled hair and finger-combed it back on both sides. Then she lifted the fallen veil from her shoulders and draped it for her.

"I've tried everything, Addie. Doctors, the rabbis, the herbalist. Even Petra, the midwife."

"Petra!" Adah exclaimed in mock horror. "She can't tell a plum from a pomegranate! How did you expect *her* to help? How much did you pay her?"

Abigail looked away, deciding whether to divulge the sum. "Three mites," she admitted. "That's all I can afford until Eli sells some more sheep."

"Three!" Adah almost shrieked. "Oh, Abbie, that's too much for common folks like us."

Abigail looked her older sister in the eye. "Adah, you just can't know what it is like. I want my husband back. I think he is...." Her voice trailed and died.

"Is what?" Adah pressed. "Is what, Abbie?"

"Is going somewhere else, because he can't sleep with me." Abigail turned away, busily wringing her garments for the second time.

"Oh, sis," Adah gasped. "Really?" All Abigail could manage was a nod. "I'm so sorry," Adah said. They stood in silence several seconds before Adah pulled her sister to her and held her fast.

"And the boys…" (her words stuttered through her sobs) "they are growing up so fast. And I can almost never hug them. And if I do, they are unclean for synagogue worship. James defies The Law and touches me anyway. But Joseph fears the rabbis and tries hard to keep The Law. It's tearing our family apart, Addie. I'm losing them. And I can't do anything about it." For a few seconds she cried against her sister's shoulder.

"Not to mention being half-sick all the time," Adah comforted gently. "Where did this awful disease come from, sis? I hate that you have it."

Abigail pulled away and wiped her eyes on her veil. "Have you heard about this Jesus who has been healing people?" she asked.

"The one who upset the rabbis when he healed old crippled Jonah at the synagogue a few weeks ago?"

"Yes. And he also healed Judith, who was unclean, and many others. Do you think there is a chance he would try to heal me?" Abigail's tone was desperate. "And they say he doesn't even charge money."

Adah considered the question carefully. "Tell you what, Abbie. We'll just go and see. I think he teaches by the lake in the middle of the day. As soon as I finish up here and spread the wash to dry, I'll come and get you; and we'll go find him. What do we have to lose?"

Abigail gave her sister one last thankful hug, balanced her basket of wet clothes on her head, and started up the hill toward her house. For the first time in months there was hope in her step.

Behind the Scene
A Study of Mark 5:21–34

The Problem of "Bothering God": Mark 5:21–29

When our sick and desperate lady reached Jesus she was met with many reasons for not bothering him with her problems. First was the crowd that engulfed him, forming a barrier to anyone needing his help. Only the strong and confident could break through it. Second was the urgent need of Jairus, whose cry had reached Jesus' ear just ahead of her own. How could a woman's chronic bleeding problem compare to the call of his dying child? Surely this could not be the time to ask Jesus for help. And Jairus was a synagogue official—a person of status, while she was just a commoner in the crowd—an unclean commoner.

Then there was the very private nature of her need. Questions would be asked, and it was against good taste to speak of such things as female menstrual problems in front of a male stranger. Most would have turned away, hoping for a more convenient time. Lastly, there was her discouragement at having been used and abused by healers of all kinds in the past. Would this Jesus be any different? Somehow she knew that he would be. Stop now and read the complete story in the passage above.

To get a better idea of what she had been dealing with these twelve years, turn back to Leviticus and read Chapter 15:19–33. The Law was very specific and unbending toward women with female disorders, hoping to protect the nation from contamination of various types. The stigma placed on a woman with an ailment such as this was a heavy burden to bear. In our "enlightened age," we choose not to take seriously some of the prohibitions against "touching the unclean thing," but in her day there was no way around compliance with The Law. In our day we can treat conditions like endometriosis, uterine cancer, or fibroid tumors with surgery, but then they had no such technology. We can only imagine what it did emotionally to families caught in this web.

Did you wonder at the conversation between Abbie and her sister about the ashes of an ostrich egg and an ass's dung with barley corns? Actually, research indicates (as confirmed by several historians) that the Jewish rabbis had ten or more "cures" for female issues, including both of the above. Some were less bizarre—more in the nature of potions and salves—but many were unbelievable to modern minds. We associate such with only the most primitive of today's cultures and find it difficult to realize that First Century Jews were subject to such beliefs.

Now "Abigail" (as we have named her) had to make a decision. When she arrived, Jesus was leaving with Jairus—hurrying toward the dying child. What could be her only chance for a cure was moving past her at a rapid pace. *Maybe I can touch his robe as he goes by,* she must have thought. *Then I won't have to bother him and delay him on his way.* Now he was past her, and all she could do was reach out to let the back of his robe—just the sleeve or the fringes—graze through her fingers from behind. Just a touch, but it was enough!

Touch Point

Can you remember a time when you had a troublesome problem but did not want to "bother God" about it? Maybe you can identify what brought you to that decision. It is possible to feel too insignificant to matter to God. Conversely, it is possible to feel too self-sufficient—as though we did not need God's help.

Either opposite can drive us to try everything else first while the situation worsens with delay. We can try medicine, science, philosophy, psychology, fads, and friends. None of these is bad or wrong—only powerless without God's working in them. Our best bet is to begin by reaching out to God, letting him lead us to whatever answer—be it miracle or medicine—that brings praise to his Name.

The Compassionate Interruption: Mark 5:30–34

Was it her touch or his power that effected the cure? It was both. If she had not reached out to a busy Lord, he would not likely have healed her. She knew instantly that she was cured (how, we do not know). And he knew instantly that he had given a cure, but to whom he did not know.

Was he irritated by the interruption? Did he scold her for delaying him? Or flinch because she was unclean? Did Jairus protest, "My daughter is dying, Master! Don't stop for anything!" No, because the Lord has time for our needs. He cares that we are sick. He hears the silent prayer and sees the secret need.

How great was her faith? Well, hers may have been small, but it doesn't take much. It was enough to cause her to seek him out when all else had failed her. It was enough to motivate her to reach out and touch Jesus when she felt he didn't have time to stop and talk. And in this story lies one of the most encouraging pictures of salvation in all the Gospels. Because now we know it doesn't take a formal response, a certain prayer of faith, a formula of words, a ceremony in a church house, to enter the Kingdom. All it takes is a desperate throwing of oneself into the path of the gracious Lord—and he does all the rest. Jesus loves our words, but he reads our hearts. What he is looking for is the simple faith that trusts him for a cure to life. This humble woman was just as whole without words as was the educated Nicodemus or the forceful John the Baptist.

Why, then, did Jesus stop on the road and call for her to come forward? Time was of the essence, and she was embarrassed. The healing was complete. Did there need to be a public recognition there on the spot? Jesus thought so, and we must look for his reasons. From that conversation came a wonderful affirmation from the Lord to this trembling new believer. "Daughter," he called her gently, "your faith has healed you. Go in peace, and be freed from your suffering." Matthew's story says, "Take heart, daughter" (see 9:22). What a lovely memory for her to treasure as she ran back to her family healed! Never would she doubt that she had truly met the Lord and experienced a superhuman cure. Her faith and his power were married publicly in that moment.

But look what the crowds would have missed if she had been let go in a secret silence. Only her closest friends and family would ever have known about the miracle or praised the Father for it. When Jesus called her forward, there for the entire world to see was another shining example of how deeply he cares about even the most private needs of our lives. Had there been time, they could have held a praise and testimony service right there on the road! A broken life had been made whole. A broken family had been given a new beginning.

Never do I read this story without remembering an early morning in 1967, soon after my father's death. In the month following his unexpected passing, my mother was pitifully ill. She suffered a mild heart attack, but her greater affliction was emotional in nature. Never a strong spirit, his death brought her near to a second mental collapse. My sister and I traded weeks staying with her those first months.

One morning early she wakened me, desperately distraught with fear and grief. She had not slept, and her anguished plea to me was, "Tell me how to be saved. I can't get through this without God." You would need to know that Mother had abandoned her faith in her teenage years. Family dysfunction and disgrace had alienated her from friends at school and church. In the next few years she met and married my father, an inactive Catholic, and they set up a family with no church ties. When my sister and I found Jesus during our youth a great struggle invaded our family life. *We*—centered on Christ and our Christian friends at church, and *they*—strongly objecting to our bringing religion into the home. For years we lived in controlled conflict, each resolute in our choices. When my sister and I both chose lives in the ministry, our parents kindly kept their objections to themselves.

Now Daddy was gone, and Mother was forced in those dawn hours to confront her spiritual emptiness. I shook off sleep and went to wash my face, silently praying, "Lord, what shall I tell her that she in her brokenness can grasp?" In that moment the Lord brought to mind this very story in Mark 5:26–28. Mother seemed so like this desperately ill woman. She had been under the care of physicians and psychiatrists for twenty years and had spent great sums of money, only to grow worse. Now, totally overcome by the circumstances of her life, she could only come and throw herself on the mercy of Jesus, touch his robe, and hope for healing.

Reaching for her dusty Bible, I read my mother this story, and then went over the basic steps to faith. Together we knelt by her bed and prayed for her to be spiritually healed and whole. And Jesus stopped on the way, turned and honored her trembling faith, and gave her peace.

Touch Point

Sometimes we grasp for formulas that make us feel secure and in control. "This is how a person is saved." "This is the right way to pray." "This plan of Bible study will work best." "A church that does it this way will grow." We seem to take comfort in believing we have found the only true answer.

In this regard, the lady in our story can help us. Like my mother, she didn't exactly walk "The Roman Road," or pray the recommended "Sinner's Prayer." Seeing how Jesus is able to work inside and outside of the mold may help us be more accepting of spiritual experiences that are not like our own have been.

Did you love the way Jesus called her "Daughter?" What a warm and loving way to receive her into the family of God! I like to think that's what he calls us, too. "Daughter…Go in peace."

Persevering in Long-Term Trials

Questions always nag us. Why are God's answers sometimes so slow in coming? Twelve years of sickness, isolation, anemia, disrupted relationships, is a very long time. And, what about the situations when healing *never* comes? When the problem persists and takes us to the grave? Even with her lengthy illness, this lady's story had a happy ending. Some—as we can all testify to—do not seem to find one.

Two other stories could interface with this one. One is Jesus' parable of the persistent widow, found in Luke 18:1–8. While it is the tale of one seeking justice in the face of harassment, the truth seems to fit. Continue to ask, if you feel your request is a worthy one, because, in time, an answer may come. Remember Elisabeth and Hannah, Sarah and Rachael, and the years each prayed for a child? In time they received answers—in God's time. *"Ask...seek...knock..."* The promise is that God will answer in the way that is best.

But, lest we mistakenly think we can always get what we ask for, like children in a candy store, recall the experience of Paul, who lived for years with a "thorn in the flesh." Wisely, God did not have him name that affliction, so that many can identify his situation with whatever ailment plagues them at length. After years of discomfort and inconvenience, praying prayers that were not granted, Paul shares his testimony in 2 Corinthians 12:7–10. The culprit actually became, for him, a cause to thank God. He could see that it kept him humble—a balance to all the tremendous spiritual victories won as he wrote insightful letters, spoke before kings and governors, and was acclaimed by a great cloud of believers. The *thorn* made him strong *in the Lord.* He could not boast of his accomplishments, because he was too weak physically to have achieved them. His condition forced him to abide in Christ for strength and let God's power flow and work through him.

In time God helped Paul compensate for his condition. He sent Luke, the kind Greek doctor, to keep him as comfortable as possible. He sent Timothy, the strong young preacher boy, to assist him, and often travel with or for him. He gave long periods of confinement and inactivity (we call it a prison sentence!) when the great physical effort of travel was not required of him. And God himself came, in the person of his Spirit and in his children, to comfort and delight the ailing apostle in later years. Paul stopped struggling with God over the issue. God blessed Paul more greatly because he endured.

It is not given us to write the script of our lives. It is forbidden us to take matters into our own hands where life and death are concerned. Most of us are asked to live out the life we are given, through the good and the bad, and do it with grace—God's grace. But if one day Jesus meets us on the way and says gently, "Daughter, your faith has healed you. Go in peace and be freed from your suffering," we will know exactly how "Abigail" felt that day.

Touch Point

Through his half-brother, James, Jesus tells us: "Blessed is the man [or woman] who perseveres under trial, because when he [she] has stood the test, he [she] will receive the crown of life that God has promised to those that love him" (James 1:12).

Do you know someone who has endured in this life, with more than her share of heartache and suffering? Have you been inspired and blessed to see a faith that endures in the hard times, and for the long haul? Take time to write a note of encouragement to that person today. Perhaps God will use your words to make her burden lighter.

Part 3

WOMEN TOUCHED BY JESUS' LATER MINISTRY

Chapter 9

Hands Full of Love

Martha of Bethany
(Luke 10:38–42)

From the ridge the view was even more spectacular than he had remembered it. To the west, Jerusalem stood shining in the noontime sun, her temple crowning Mt. Zion. Beyond it stood Herod's palace, Antonia, and the other familiar buildings of the great city. Thomas watched as Jesus stood silent for several minutes, taking in the panorama thoughtfully.

To the east, the Olivet ridge dropped off quickly into the Jordan wilderness and the valley through which they had come. Bethany was just behind them, and far beyond it one could almost make out the oasis of Jericho, with the Salt Sea to its south.

The climb up from Jericho had taken the entire morning, and they were exhausted. Crowded as the road was with pilgrims headed for the feast, the usual fear of bandits was blessedly absent. But the climb itself had left them all spent. Of course it would not have been necessary to leave the road and hike clear up to this ridge, but Jesus seemed to want this moment, and the men tried to please him in every way they could. So they had added climb to climb. The scene helped refresh them. The women had chosen to wait for them on the road below.

Actually, the plan was that Jesus would find lodging in the village of Bethany while the others went the remaining distance into the city for the beginning of the feast week. It seemed a wise decision since the Jewish leaders were bent on his destruction and his presence in the temple could not be defended by unarmed men—which, for the most part, they were. Meanwhile, everyone had found a patch of shade in which to rest and munch a little on the remaining rations. Jesus walked down the ridge a short way in thoughtful solitude.

After a few minutes, Thomas approached him quietly. "Master?" Jesus turned and nodded. "Would you like for Matthew and me to go back to Bethany with you and show you where this Martha woman lives? We know the house. The others could go on, and we'll catch up with them."

Jesus seemed almost relieved by his offer, and Thomas went back to inform Matthew and the rest of this new plan. In the discussion that followed—and there were always plenty of opinions in the group—it was decided that all of them would make the short backtrack to Bethany and so remove the problem of being separated and trying to regroup in a city root-bound with feast-day confusion.

Peter whistled a signal, and everyone struggled to his feet, grabbing a last swig of water, then stowing flasks and gear for the remaining journey. The downhill trek to Bethany was easy compared to the morning's ambitious climb. Thomas and Matthew led the way. Bethany had been their assignment when the seventy-two went out preaching. Among the families that had received them well was the household of Martha, with her brother Lazarus and their younger sister, Mary. It was because of Martha's enthusiastic invitation to return and bring their Master that they now were placing Jesus there. Hers would be a sort of *safe house* for him during the feast. Word had gone ahead that they were coming, and she was expecting them today.

Taking Thomas' cue, the group turned off on the second road after the weeping field and continued along a row of humble houses. Goats and chickens ran about the yards and in and out of open doorways with the children. Citizens stared as the group of strangers straggled past. Thomas motioned toward a finer home just ahead on the right. Jesus stopped to converse with him briefly as the group caught up. Then Thomas and Matthew went on ahead to announce their arrival. Murmurings of approval whispered through the group as they admired the lovely home that would be their base for the holiday week.

Thomas and Matthew emerged shortly with a ma-tronly lady, who was wiping her hands on her apron as she talked. "Master, this is Martha, the lady of the house," Matthew said, smiling. "Martha, this is Jesus, our Teacher, and the rest of our group." Martha bowed low, holding her veil over her mouth and nose, but friendly eyes gave her away.

A slim, younger man bounded out of the house towards them and Matthew introduced him as her younger brother, Lazarus. The usual Hebrew greeting was spoken around. "Forgive my tardiness," Lazarus explained. I was just tying the lamb to the spit. My sister is the best cook in the village, and if I did the job right we'll be in for a treat when we return from the temple tonight."

Jesus accompanied Martha into the house, followed by Matthew, James, and Lazarus, who brought the baggage to deposit for safekeeping. Lazarus ducked out the back and returned quickly, shouldering a live lamb for the sacrifice. He joined the others and they were off for Jerusalem and the feast. Jesus watched them leave, then turned to his hostess for instructions.

"Lazarus has put up the tabernacle for feast days." she offered. "Here, it's in the courtyard. I'll show you the way." They went out the side door and into a walled stone patio surrounded by flowering vines and shrubs. A private well stood to one side. The tabernacle was large, held by several strong uprights, and covered on the top and sides with newly cut branches, their leaves still green.

"Your brother does good work," Jesus admired. "He is a good man."

"I think you will like it out here," Martha said. "This is where we eat and sleep during the feast days. The weather has been perfect. A gentle breeze blows down off the mountain most afternoons." She gestured toward the wide front opening of the booth.

Jesus stooped to enter but was startled by a young woman sitting inside on a mat, absorbed in the task of mending a garment.

"This is my younger sister, Mary," Martha said, and Mary rose to bow low at her words. "She is the third member of the family. We are all that are left since our mother passed on two years ago now."

Jesus returned Mary's smile and found a comfortable seat across from her.

"Now, if I may be excused, I need to check the lamb and see to the evening meal. There is much to do if we are to have fourteen hungry men to feed." Martha bowed before the great teacher and started to leave, then turned with some last words for her sister. "Now, Mary, do not talk the Master's ears off. He needs to rest. And remember, in just a little while I will need your help with the table and chores. The vegetables must be cooked and the bread baked—and the lamb will require continual attention. With Lazarus gone, you will need to milk the ewes before supper. I know it doesn't sound like much, but it all adds up, and I can't do it all by myself."

Mary responded compliantly as her sister quickly left. Then she looked at Jesus, who had listened solemnly through the lecture, and laughed softly. "She is *so* fussy about her meals. Really—she is a *very* good cook—her meals are spectacular. Lazarus and I try to help, but we are never able to please her. It's like, she's the mother and we are the children." Mary offered him a pillow for his back, and they both settled comfortably under the arbor.

"Now, Sir," she said to Jesus, "I know I am just a woman, but—if you are not too tired from your travels, I would like so much to hear some of the wonderful things you have been teaching. Lazarus was so impressed with your Disciples when they visited with us. Would it be all right for a woman to know the things of God, also?" As she talked, she passed Jesus a tray of olives, dried figs, and cheese. "Bethany is well-known for its figs, you know," she said with a smile.

Jesus looked at the bright young lass before him for a long moment. "What would you like to hear?" he asked.

Behind the Scene
A Study of Luke 10:38–42

How Did They Meet? Luke 11:38

There is so much to love in this story! And so many missing answers! This seems to be the first time Jesus came in contact with this very special Bethany family—at least it is the first *recorded* event. It could have been "quite by accident" that the Disciples and Jesus happened into town and were invited to stay in Martha's home. On feast weeks it was not uncommon for Jerusalem to be filled to the brim, and the small villages of the surrounding area picked up the overflow of bed and breakfast guests.

Several researchers have put this story into the same week as the one we'll study next in John 7 and 8, the woman taken in adultery. Because John chose to tell different stories about Jesus' ministry than those in Luke, the two accounts are sometimes difficult to interface. We can know that both this visit to Bethany and the Feast of Tabernacles (John 7:2) happened in the fall of the year. Some Bible scholars see in John 7:10–14 the perfect place to insert the Bethany event. Because of Jewish opposition, Jesus remained in the area but not in Jerusalem proper. It also gives us a reason for Lazarus not being introduced in this Bible passage. He would have been at the feast. Also, Luke 10:38 seems to indicate that Jesus alone remained at Bethany. "She opened her house to *him*" not to *them*. So the probability works well with our logic.

Still have your Sherlock Holmes hat on? How did Martha hear of Jesus to begin with, and what caused her to trust him and invite him to stay there? Simply put, God opened her heart. God uses circumstances and people to make ready the hearts of those he needs. In Luke 9:51–53 we were told that Jesus was bound for Jerusalem, and that he spent some time in Samaria. Then Luke 10:1 begins the account of Jesus sending seventy-two of his disciples out to prepare the villages to which he would go, apparently for a Judean crusade. Bible scholars think Bethany may have been one of those villages, and that some or all of Martha's household came into contact with Jesus' people at that time. We have surmised in our story that some of those disciples were well-received by Martha, and so decided to bring Jesus to her for these few days of hiding out before he went to the feast.

Allow us one more speculation. It was not usual for women to own property in that day. Why was the house Martha's and not her brother's? If this story were longer, we could build a case for Martha being the widow of a wealthy lawyer, or some such. That would explain the house not going to her brother as the male heir, or to all three siblings equally. In any case, Martha seems definitely to be the head of the household.

Touch Point

One of the strongest things going for Martha was her willingness to get involved in the Kingdom—to take a risk. Her strength was hospitality, and that became her vehicle for serving. The world can be a scary place, and it is far safer and easier to go inside our comfortable homes, close and lock the doors, and draw our families around us, shutting out others, than to invite people in. Martha answered the call to let Jesus into her home and thus opened a wonderful chapter in the lives of the Bethany three.

Hospitality is such a wonderful gift of the Spirit! And every woman does not have it naturally, as Martha did, obviously. Hebrews 13:2 has this wonderful and curious admonition: "Do not forget to entertain strangers, for by so doing some people have entertained angels without knowing it." A warm and loving home opens itself and its family to great

blessings as God feels free to send his special messengers—perhaps not angelic, but special nonetheless—there to be refreshed. Paul indicates that hospitality, while sometimes a gift, can also be a learned skill (see Romans 12:13). And Peter echoes this in I Peter 4:9. Spiritual gifts are never designated male or female, but as women we can certainly resonate with this home-centered, positive attribute.

The Personality Contrast: Luke 10:39–40

We cannot contain all our amusement at the struggle between the sisters, while knowing from our own lives that sister squabbles can be very hurtful. For some reason, Martha had a big dinner to prepare. In our story we have assumed that all the menfolk would be walking the two miles back from Jerusalem that evening, arriving late and hungry. If it was the Feast of Tabernacles, as we have proposed, that would further explain the elaborate preparations.

How many times did Martha come to the courtyard door and call for Mary before she got exasperated enough to speak to Jesus about it? How many of Mary's chores did Martha do, while she built her head of steam from irritation to resentment to overt anger? How many times before this day had Mary found a way to stonewall when there was work to be done? It isn't likely this problem was an isolated incident, but more of an ongoing family situation.

And there was the matter of needing the acceptance and admiration of a rabbi so famous as Jesus. Mary was monopolizing his time and attention. A wonderful rapport was building between them, but Martha was being ignored and left to do the work unappreciated. And what was Mary doing in the company of a man, talking *synagogue talk,* anyway? Women and men were generally not even encouraged to speak together in Jewish culture, and women were never formally taught the Scriptures. Mary's protracted visit with Jesus was unseemly by the standards of Jewish women.

At some point Martha's self control boiled dry and she marched right into the conversation and brought the sore point to a head. Incredibly, she laid part of the blame squarely on the honored guest. "Lord, don't you care…?" *Could you get involved here?* "Tell her to help me!" She laid the rest of it right in Mary's lap. "…my sister has left me to do all the work by myself." The inequity was perfectly clear to Martha. Why were the other two so oblivious? To her credit, Martha didn't keep things bottled up inside, did she? She went straight to the source, looked the two offenders in the eye, and spoke her piece.

Now, if we can put a stop-action on that scene and look to the larger truths, we can know that God did not make these two sisters—or any two sisters—alike. They had different personalities. Martha was a doer, a planner, an organizer, and a good hostess (see John 12:2). She may have been the Martha who gave Martha Stewart her name! Mary was probably a quieter type, more introverted, more studious (compare John 12:3). Their spiritual abilities were not alike. We would classify Martha as having the gifts of hospitality and serving.

Mary's gifts included devotion and generosity. Neither did God love one lady more than the other. We are told in the occasion of their second meeting, the death of their brother, "Jesus loved Martha and her sister and Lazarus." (John 11:5)

Touch Point

Have you noticed how many families have continuing conflict even after the children are adults? Some of it is a carry-over from childhood. First children are always first, and often resented for it. Second children are always playing catch-up and never get over it. There comes a time when we must assume our adulthood, however, and turn loose of old feelings in the interest of building a family of love and unity. Sometimes that is easier said than done.

Funny how much it helps to raise children of our own. So many of the imagined injustices of our childhood melt away as we struggle to avoid the same pitfalls in our own parenting. How often we have an "Aha!" moment when we say, "I finally understand why my mom let that happen. This job isn't as easy as it looked from the kneecaps up."

Part of growing up whole is accepting that we are all very different and unique, and it is supposed to be that way. Then, upon coming to that place, we begin to be free to really take

pride in who our siblings have become and to move from nipping at their heels to cheering them on. That's progress!

The other part of that is deciding to accept and like who I am. God didn't make me like the sister I've always compared myself to, because he designed me to be who I am. Psalm 139 has many wonderful thoughts that make us glad to be the person God designed us to be. I like verses 1–4 and 13–19 especially well on this. As regards handling old resentments and misunderstandings, verses 23-24 are a brave and healing prayer.

Loving Them Both: Luke 10:41–42

Jesus was happy to be a guest in the home, and to enjoy Martha's hospitality and good cooking. After days on the road, probably camping out, it was, no doubt, a welcome reprieve to be in a private home. He did not fault Martha for who she was or for what she was doing, but chided the spirit that motivated her. Where would we be without the Marthas among us to run our church kitchens, entertain our visiting evangelists, and keep our buildings clean and lovely? Praise God for the Marthas of our fellowships! Marthas love Jesus as much as Marys, but they bake their love into cakes and casseroles.

We see Martha in the gals who pray on the run, serve God by serving others, jump in to chair the committee or teach the children's choir, deliver meals to the sick, cook revival and funeral lunches, rescue us when nobody planned things right, and are quick to give us a shoulder to lean on.

But Jesus needed even more what Mary was offering at that moment—a quiet respite from a life that was growing more dangerous and stressful with each day. What they discussed that afternoon we do not know, but from that point onward, Jesus and Mary had an empathy that is beautiful to see. It was her tears that moved him to groan and sob at her brother's tomb (see John 11:32–35). It was her nard and her tears that encouraged him as he faced death (John 12:3 and 7). They became soulmates for the remaining few months of his ministry on earth.

Jesus' answer to Martha is classic: "Martha, Martha, dear friend... you are fussing and worrying so...." She needed to hear from him that her work was seen and valued. She also needed some perspective. She could have dropped the *Jewish mama* routine that holiday. It would have been an excellent night for a sandwich meal—something simple. Martha had seen it as a night to shine, however, and had put her pride on the line. In modern vernacular, he might have said, "Can we just use paper plates instead of the good china?"

By contrast, he gently defended Mary's choice. She honored him with her heart, while Martha honored him with her hands. In that hour, spiritual food was a higher priority with Jesus than banquet food. Mary would not have another opportunity to sit and talk with Jesus in quite this way. And so—final answer—he did not honor Martha's request to send Mary to the kitchen.

What do you think happened next? Did Martha go off sulking to do the best she could with no help? Did Mary shorten her conversation with Jesus and go help her sister after all? Did the meal get on the table reasonably well-prepared? Or did Martha leave the pots, join them in the arbor, and let the lamb burn on the spit? Wouldn't it be fun to tune in for next week's episode? Verses like John 12:2 and 3 assure us that Martha continued to be Martha, and Mary continued to be Mary. And in John 11:5 we find comfort that Jesus continued to love and value them both.

Truth be known, most of us would like not to be either a Martha or a Mary, but some combination of the two. There is a danger in being a Mary. While Marys pray, study, worship, and share, the house can get pretty dirty, and the laundry can overflow the hamper. Some Marys use their devotion as an excuse to avoid the practical duties of life, to the frustration of their husbands and families. So also is there a danger in being a Martha. Marthas can become so distracted with getting the job done that they substitute working for worshiping, disregard sensitive feelings in others, and grow blase' about spiritual things. They measure their devotion by the tasks accomplished and get too busy *serving* Jesus to spend time *talking* with him. No, let's not be either a Martha or a Mary, but rather, cultivate the best of both. Let's love Jesus with both our hearts and our hands!

Touch Point

I guess we all strive with difficulty for the well-balanced life. There are so many keys in this story that give us clues to getting there. Notice some of these:

- There is the matter of identifying our gifts and abilities, and making the most of them;
- And, conversely identifying our weaknesses and shortcomings, and working on them;
- There is a freedom to be ourselves, knowing God designed us and loves us as we are;
- And a suggestion that we allow others the same freedom, and celebrate who they are;
- There is an admonition to seize the moment with God, not missing one-time opportunities for spiritual growth and service;
- And an admonition for living with one foot on the ground, not losing touch with the practical realities and duties of life.

Self improvement! It's so much better when it comes in the gentle Presence of Jesus. Let's build a tabernacle...and spend a few hours there!

Chapter 10

Set Free

The Woman Accused of Adultery
(John 8:2–11)

The afternoon breeze blew in heavy with the smell of freshly cut grain. Philippa lay back on a makeshift pillow and looked at the Tishri sky through the thatch of the arbor. This was her favorite week of the year, the celebration of the ancestors' pilgrimage through the desert. Many people camped out in their yards, sleeping and eating in tabernacles, keeping cooking simple, and feasting with family and relatives. All her children would be home tomorrow, but this evening she and Aaron had made plans with friends. Or…*she* had made plans that Aaron would know about when he got in from the temple.

Simple food for the evening meal was warming in the courtyard oven. A hearty stew, fresh bread, a basket of autumn fruits, and some of Aaron's good wine would be just fine for their guests. Old friends like Jonna and Solomon come for the conversation, not for elaborate fare. Aaron would enjoy Solomon's company, and she and Jonna were long overdue for a good visit.

Wispy clouds floated overhead, weaving themselves through the thatch like tufts of whitened wool. As she watched, Philippa's thoughts drifted back to the wrenching conversation she had had with Mary Sarah as they walked home from the market this morning. All day the story had come and gone in her mind as she went about her tasks. She had always thought so much of Mary Sarah and Nicolas. She'd never even considered that his life might have a darker side. *Poor Sarah! How does one handle finding out such a sad thing?* She hoped never to have to know.

A door shut. Aaron was home from the temple and would come looking for her shortly in the usual way. When he emerged into the courtyard a few minutes later, he had two cups of wine in his hands and a tight smile on his lips. "Oh, oh!" She responded. "Did you have a hard day?"

He shook his head unconvincingly as he ducked under the canopy and settled onto a cushion beside her. "Not bad, Phil. It was just such a madhouse at the temple with all the pilgrims and animals running here and there, and the vendors working overtime. With my bad hearing, I barely had an understandable conversation all day."

"Wish we could do something more about that," she sympathized, taking the cup he offered.

"And this Jesus controversy is heating up. Today he made the most outlandish promises to the people, and—poor dullards that they are—they just lapped it up like honey wine."

Philippa had been following the Jesus saga for months now. "What kind of outlandish promises?"

"Like, that he is from God and will go back to God soon. Crazy stuff!" Aaron complained.

"That's almost blasphemy," Philippa protested. "Didn't someone try to stop him?"

"And," Aaron interrupted, "that he has some kind of *water* that will quench people's thirst for the rest of their lives—whatever that is supposed to mean."

"Why hasn't the council stopped him?" Philippa demanded again. "Crazy people need to be pulled off the steps and locked up before they do harm to the unlearned who don't know any better than to believe."

"Well," Aaron shifted to his elbow and adjusted his tunic as he struggled to explain. "We tried. The Council tried. But he has citizen's rights, you know. We sent the guards, but they all came back thoroughly intimidated by the man's intellect and charisma. It just dumbfounded us all." He paused for a sip before continuing. "And even one of our own, Nicodemus, practically defended him."

Philippa shook her head. "That man needs to be stopped," she repeated.

A few seconds of silence elapsed, then Philippa changed the subject. "I heard a really sad story today from Mary Sarah, coming back from the market. One of those things you'd rather not know."

"What was that?" Aaron asked. "Or would I rather not know?"

"Apparently she's suspected Nicolas of playing around on her for some time, and last week she had him followed. He went to the inn on Bethany Road to watch the new dancer, but the fuller—the man she paid to follow him—said after the dancing and all that, he spent most of the night with the girl. Mary Sarah is just devastated."

"Nicolas?" Aaron asked, surprised. "Well, that old fool! I didn't know he had that much fire left." Then, noting her frown, he took another route. "I'm sure Mary Sarah is hurt. Is the girl pretty?"

"Yes, I think so. But the point is…" Philippa refocused, "it's also wrong, and she is trying to decide whether there is anything she can do about it. I'm afraid she's probably just stuck with her secret. No one would believe her if she told them, anyway."

They sipped their wine together and watched a pair of swallows swooping overhead. "Did she say if the dancer is married?" Aaron asked.

"Betrothed to some poor harvest hand, which is just as bad. I wonder what your *Jesus person* would say about adultery?" Philippa mused. "Would he go for the stoning, or for the pardoning? Stoning a pretty, young girl would ruin his popularity with the silly crowds that seem to believe him. But pardoning would put him against Moses and the Law. That's somewhere between a rock and a hard place, seems to me."

Aaron pondered the puzzle, then sat bolt up in the booth. "You know, Phil—that just might be the trap we are looking for! Good girl! Good thinking!" And he gave her leg a friendly pat. "If we could catch old Nicolas and that girl…what's her name?"

"I think Sarah called her Jacintha, or something like that." Philippa's wrinkled brow showed she hadn't caught what he had in mind.

"If we could catch old Nicolas and Jacintha, or whoever she is, in the bed together—right in the act of it—and bring them to Jesus to judge, he would have to prove himself, right in front of his adoring throngs. And any answer he gave would be wrong. Now, how could we do that?" His enthusiasm surprised her. He was more determined about this Jesus than she had realized.

"I guess someone could go to the inn during the night?" she offered. "Mary Sarah's spy would know which room the girl uses. But, you know, Aaron, you wouldn't even need to catch Nicolas. For Sarah's sake you could just let him slip away. Just find them together and bring in the girl. If she's very young and pretty the crowd will care more what you do with a pretty dancer than with an old goat like him."

"This gets better by the minute," he responded. "Then, if this Jesus calls for stoning, the people will hate him for taking the hard road. And if he calls for pardoning…"

"…the people will see he is a fake who doesn't keep The Law, and then you can take him in for blasphemy," she finished. "Oh! I forgot to tell you in all this distraction! Solomon and Jonna are due for dinner in just a little while. I hope that is all right?" she asked.

"Good! That's good!" Aaron responded. "Sol can help me think this thing out. If he likes the idea, we can have Caiaphas send the temple guards in the night tonight, and have them, or *her*, caught before dawn." He ducked under the arbor doorway, standing tall and pleased before her. "With any luck we'll have her in front of Jesus by dawn—and haul him into the Council on a charge before noon."

Philippa hadn't seen him so happy in many weeks. "It's worth a try," she agreed, reaching up so he could help her stand. "Now, let's get ready for Solomon and Jonna. Would you get the wineskin and two more cups while I check the stew?" And they hurried off in two directions like kids with a secret.

Behind the Scene
A Study of John 8:2–11

A Stir in the Temple

The Feast of Tabernacles (or Booths) was in full swing. Joyous pilgrims wandered throughout the temple grounds—celebrating the recent harvest, offering sacrifices, and remembering their ancestors' forty-year journey through the wilderness. Makeshift booths and shelters were in every yard and patio, and neighbor called to neighbor as families camped outside for the eight-day, Octoberfest. Some feast days were solemn occasions, but the Feast of Booths was a happy time of celebrating harvest and heritage.

Jesus came to the Jerusalem area early (this is thought to be the time when he met and stayed with Martha and her family in Bethany, as told in Luke 10:38), but he determined not to go to the feast until about midway through it (see John 7:10–14). By then, the crowds would be dense, and his presence would be more protected. Already he was a wanted man. It was about six months before his Crucifixion.

The story of the feast itself, and Jesus' many confrontations with the crowds and the Jewish religious leaders, is told in some detail in John 7:1–52 and 8:12–59. The entire conflict centered on one very vital question: *Was Jesus truly the Messiah, or was he an hallucinating impostor?* Three groups of people were puzzling over the problem. First, the pilgrims who had come in from the surrounding country and Galilee, many of whom were familiar with Jesus' miracles and teachings. Some of them believed in him. They had seen the proof. Second, the Jewish leaders, alarmed by his popularity and influence with the people, were determined to rid the nation of such as he. Their entire system of religion and their livelihood were threatened. And lastly, the Jewish citizens from Jerusalem who were caught in the middle—seeing the miracles, but also aware of how their religious leaders felt. These hesitated to pin their hopes on a wanted man. Everyone was hanging on Jesus' every word—some for what they could learn about God and some in the hope that he would mis-speak and condemn himself.

Touch Point

Always we seem to have the struggle of official religion and its educated leaders versus the crowd of lay worshipers who try to listen with their hearts. How is one to know whether those with the recognized dogma or paradigm are the closer match to God's intent? How does a believer properly interact with church professionals when there is a question of direction or theology to be decided?

Those of us in the "profession" of religion, it seems to me, must continually check our motives, asking ourselves questions such as...*Is this a personal power struggle or a scriptural fence to guard? Am I actually afraid for my job or my name? Am I defending a manmade barricade to faith? Is there a reluctance to leave my comfort zone, or could the Spirit be motivating this way of God's moving? Am I judging too quickly? Is there a personality conflict at the base of this? Am I just reluctant to share leadership?*

The most telling questions might be these: *If Jesus were to come into my church today, would I welcome his message and his ways? What if he taught and demonstrated insights that went contrary to my thinking? Am I an "old wineskin"—unable to accept the fresh, new, expansive filling of his Spirit?*

172

God, help us to bend where we need to bend, change where we need to change, and hold fast where we need to hold fast.

Pinning Down the Story

This story of Jesus and the woman taken in adultery has a life of its own. For the first half of the first millennium A.D., historians tell us it did not appear in John's gospel at all. Often, if it *was* included, it was attached to Luke 21:38. Scholars say it is more in the style of Luke's writings than John's. That is, it uses Greek words that Luke used, not those typical of the writings of John. Though most scholars feel the story is authentic, but possibly misplaced, others reject it. (It has been treated as a questionable passage by both the Revised Standard Version and the New English Bible). But for our purposes, we will just leave it where it is—in John's account of the feast. To the devotional reader, it seems to fit there as well as anywhere.

What *is* obvious is this: the entire disgraceful episode was set up by the Jewish leaders as a trap. Jesus' popularity with the crowds prevented them from hauling him out of the temple and doing away with him. Their hope was that he would condemn himself in some way, so they could involve the Romans and call for the death penalty for him. To do this, they needed to turn the tide of public favor, and that was not going to be an easy thing to do.

And Where Was the Man?: John 8:2–6

So much is contrived and calloused about this story. Have you taken time to read it from the Bible yet? As many have pointed out, there was no need to drag the accused woman before the crowd. They could have held her in custody while explaining the problem to Jesus. Instead, calling her out was a predetermined act meant to arouse the people and advertise the event publicly. No thought was shown here for her feelings, her already tarnished reputation, her needs. They *used* her, plain and simple. In our society, even criminals have rights, but loose Jewish women were low on the stack pole of respect.

We must take care not to diminish the seriousness of the crime of adultery. Yes, in the Bible *it is* a crime, punishable by death. As were the crimes of blaspheming God's Name and character, worshiping false gods, desecrating the day of worship, sacrificing humans (does that include fetuses?) and dabbling in occult practices. If those standards held up in American courts, we would be more dead than alive, I fear.

Touch Point

We need to consider from where our morality comes today. Paul warned us in Romans 12:1–3 that we should strive for holiness of body and mind, not conforming to the world or looking to common wisdom for our patterns. But many actions specifically forbidden

in God's Word seem to be quite acceptable to us now as Christians.

Man's law is not always the same as God's law and often falls short of the ideals set for us in Scripture. God's Word clearly teaches us that sexual promiscuity is not allowable with God. A question for us could be: Do I really want to live a holy lifestyle and be noticeably different from my peers at work and at play? Or, am I striving for the "acceptable"—some lesser spiritual level that will keep the convicting of the Spirit off my back while allowing me to be "tolerant" in whatever crowd I choose to travel?

If the answer points toward holiness, we can never let the world around us decide what is the "good, acceptable, and perfect will of God." That standard is defined in God's Word.

All the teachings of The Law demanded death for both partners involved in adultery. Check Leviticus 20:7, and 10–13 for a list of such offenses. The manner of death is not directed in that passage. Old Testament Israelites allowed capital punishment by stoning, strangulation, and burning in different situations. However, the parallel passage in Deuteronomy 22:22–29 commanded stoning for adultery or rape under certain conditions. But note that the *man* carries the greater blame. All of this was designed by God to keep his people pure and uphold the sanctity of marriage, and the laws that make society work best. This leads us back to the question: Why was the man allowed to slip away and remain anonymous and blameless? It all points to the rulers contriving the situation, and bending their sacred Law in a way that would best achieve their goals.

Now, to complicate things a bit more, in the time of Jesus, the Romans *were* the law, and they did not allow the Jewish leaders to impose a death penalty. Roman courts held the determination about capital punishment. So, had the Jews been successful in getting Jesus to rule for stoning, the punishment could not have been carried out in a location so closely observed. Apparently stoning still occurred in places where the Roman authorities were not watching, because both Jesus and Paul narrowly escaped it, and Stephen met his death in that way at the hands of the Jews.

Between a Rock and a Hard Place: John 8:6–9

This passage has always piqued my imagination, because it is possibly the only one that shows Jesus writing. Why did he stoop and write? Was he thinking? Ignoring? Angry? Embarrassed? An old Hollywood movie suggested, rather insightfully, that he was writing out the sins of those close enough to read the words. We would like to know what he wrote, and what they read into it, but the Bible does not include this detail.

Nevertheless, the accusers continued to shoot questions and comments until Jesus stood back up, looked them squarely in the eye, and gave his ruling. "OK, stone her as the Law requires, but only those of you who have not done—or wished to do—the same thing may begin the execution" (this writer's loose translation). Remember, Jesus taught that, "anyone who looks at a woman lustfully has already committed adultery with her in his heart" (Matthew 5:28). And he also taught: "for in the same way you judge others, you will be judged, and with the measure you use, it will be measured to you" (Matthew 7:2). And again he stooped to write in the dirt, letting the words fall on hearts as they would.

We are told by the writer that fists opened, stones dropped to the ground, and one by one the men who were spoiling for a lynching just walked away. Why the *elder* first and the *younger* last? Maybe it was human nature. Younger ones fire up more quickly when mob rule takes charge. But the elders had more years in which to experience the sins of passion. Probably for many reasons, to a man they just melted from the scene. The Council's schemes had failed again.

The Real Verdict: John 8:10–11

Then it was just two of them and the crowd. Jesus turned to look directly at this one who had been so terribly disgraced and humiliated before her world, and now spoke his heart. "Woman," he began. It wasn't a harsh word, but one of respect and kindness. "Where did they all go? Did no one stay to carry out the sentence?" He knew, but he needed for her to admit to herself that she had been set free. Guilt is such a devastating and dogging kind of baggage to haul with us. Self esteem is so very difficult to rebuild. Here on the sand that had been his writing tablet he began to lay a new foundation for her life.

"Then I don't condemn you, either. But you need to leave your sinful life and start over."

Carefully, Jesus did not condone her unlawful relationship outside of marriage. He had utmost respect for God's laws, and had taught against adultery on other occasions, as we have already noted. Instead, he gently gave her a plan for a new and lawful life. Those are freeing words, friends! *You can start over!*

Sins of passion are so common about us that we scarcely know when we are crossing the line into the quicksand of compromise. Unmarried sex is as common as every prime time TV and movie script, and cheating pulses through nearly every music station. In the secret of their bedrooms, people search the Internet for conversations with anonymous, debased minds. Filthy magazines and clubs allow deviations we can scarcely conceive of. Those who struggle to live by God's laws are considered oddities by their neighbors, and sometimes by their own kids. Parents have good cause to fear that their children will hear and believe the world's view of morality before they can understand what God is saying to them in his Word.

Sometimes we come home from the world at the end of the day knowing we have been sucked in. And then the demons set in and have a field day, showing us how miserably we have failed, how ruined we are. At those times we can come before the Lord, confessing, and hear him say, *"No one has the right to condemn you. And I don't condemn you. But you need to leave that sin and start over."*

Touch Point

It works the opposite way, also. Sometimes we are the sinners, but sometimes we try to be the accusers. We need to keep checking our hands to see if we have picked up rocks to throw at those who are living outside God's laws. Jesus set us the pattern when he carefully did not condone the *behavior*, but was kind and redemptive toward the *person*. We may need to begin a rock pile outside the door of our own lives, where we can deposit the stones we've picked up in righteous indignation. People who are caught in a life of sin have enough bruises without our adding pain to pain.

Did you read about the controversial priest in New York City who was helping prostitutes by paying for their housing, childcare, and job training so that they could get off the street and get a new start? Amazingly, he was soundly criticized by "rights" groups for making these women feel ashamed of their lives! The shame was already there. God has built it into us and called it a *conscience*. The priest was offering them a way out; in effect saying: "I don't condemn you, either. But you need to leave your sinful lifestyle and start over." That idea has its *Jesus-shoes* on!

Chapter 11

Small Blessings

Mothers of the Little Children
(Matthew 19:13–15)

"He is outside the village now, by the well," she said, lifting the heavy water jar from her headpiece carefully, and lowering it to its place on the floor. Ruth was still breathless from hurrying home with the burden. "Teaching and healing…and the crowd is getting larger very fast. Everyone is going."

"Why would we want to be part of that kind of thing?" Jesse responded, moving quickly to help her balance the sloshing jug. "Fighting a crowd of people is not my favorite way to spend a day. And it's a pretty cold out there."

"I just thought—well, the baby is almost a year now, and it is time for his blessing." Ruth's tone told him she was earnest. "It isn't often a famous rabbi visits Beth

181

Nimrah, and I just felt that this was a special time for Baby David. Oh, Jesse, let's not miss this blessing!"

Jesse coiled the rope he had been braiding and called reluctantly, "Hannah and Thomas, get cleaned up. We are taking the baby to see the rabbi."

"Good!" Hannah responded, but Thomas was nowhere in sight. "Mama, may I wear my new dress that Grandma Eva made for me? I want to look nice for the rabbi." A nod sent her scurrying toward the clothes chest to find her favorite purple frock.

"Also find your woven shawl, Hannah," her mother added. "Like your father said, it's pretty cool today." Turning, she glanced around the room looking for her middle child. "Where is Thomas?"

"He's in the shed with the new baby goat," Hannah reported. "Probably dirty as ever."

Jesse stepped to the door and called him in. "Son, we are going to take the baby to the rabbi for a blessing. You need to get changed and washed." Then, almost without looking he added, "No, don't bring the goats."

A bundle of three-year-old exuberance bounded in the door, and ran past his mother giggling. Life was always a game to Thomas.

"Thomas!" Jesse said more sternly. "Stop playing, and let your mother get you ready."

Ruth drew her little son close, and began the job of washing his dusty face and hair, and pulling off the dirty clothes. "Look, son," she said, reaching into the chest, "you can wear the new tunic I made for you from Grandpa's blue robe." Fabric was hard to come by, and Ruth had seen an opportunity in reusing the good portion of one of the garments that had belonged to her father.

"Papa gone?" Thomas asked, his little face unusually serious.

"Yes, Grandpa is gone," Ruth answered. "We miss him," she sighed, continuing the tasks at hand.

"What are you going to wear to see the rabbi, Mama?" Hannah asked. "Will you wear the white dress I like so much?"

"Yes, I thought so," Ruth answered, smiling at her little daughter's attentions.

"And the pretty veil with gold ornaments?" Hannah persisted.

"I guess so," her mother responded. "Would you find my good shawl, Hannah? I'll need it to wrap the baby."

Meanwhile, Jesse was pulling on his favorite, comfortable brown tunic and goatskin shoes. "You kids sit down somewhere and stay clean while your mother dresses herself and the baby," he admonished. "No more playing now with your best clothes on."

"New shoes!" Thomas sang as he saw his father tying his on. "I have new shoes, too."

"Yours aren't new," Hannah argued. "Jonathan gave them to you because he outgrew them."

"Now Hannah," Ruth corrected, "they are new to us, and still very good. We can call them Thomas's new shoes if we like."

"But they aren't," she insisted, with five-year-old authority.

"Sister, watch your mouth," Jesse scolded his daughter quietly. "Let's not show the rabbi our worst behavior." He was tying on his belt, and securing a bag with a few coins and a small knife. Best to go prepared, he thought.

"We should take some water along, and maybe a few loaves, in case the babies need them," Ruth suggested over the heads of the children, pulling on her best dress as she spoke. "If you can get those, I'll change David's shirt and diaper, and we can be on our way."

Jesse nodded as he pulled his camel hair coat off the shelf.

"What can I take to the rabbi as a present, Mama?" Hannah asked. "Would he like this handkerchief I wove at Grandma Eva's last week?" She was pulling a piece of white cloth from the shelf behind the lamp.

Ruth smiled at her daughter, growing up so fast. "I think he would like that, Hannah. You did very nice work, for a first time at the loom."

"Me too," wailed Thomas. "I take a present too!"

"The handkerchief will be enough, Son," Ruth responded, but to no avail.

"No!" Hannah insisted. "The handkerchief is just from me, because I made it myself."

Thomas grabbed for the cloth, but his sister was too quick, and he was left empty handed and more than a little upset. "Maaa-maaa!" he cried pitifully, "Sissy won't share." Hearing him, the baby wailed back in sympathy.

"Hush!" One word from their father settled the fuss, but Thomas continued to pout and whimper.

"We'll find you something to take," Ruth comforted. "Just don't upset the baby. Now, let's get on the path before the crowds get any worse." She picked David up with one hand, and grabbed a napkin with the other. "Here, Thomas, tuck this cloth into your belt in case you need a napkin later. Don't wipe your hands on your good tunic. And let's get on your head square, because the wind is cool today. Hannah, put on your good scarf."

"Are we about ready?" Jesse asked, walking over to open the cottage door.

"I think so," Ruth responded, wrapping David in her shawl.

Taking the baby from her, Jesse went first out the door, stopping to touch the parchment and kiss his fingers in the usual way. "Look, David," he said, taking a chubby right fist in his big hand, "Kiss the *Shema* with Papa," and he guided the baby's fingers to the parchment, and then to his little lips reverently. David squealed with delight at the ritual he had already come to know.

"Lift me, Mama," Thomas begged, and Ruth boosted her son so he could touch the sacred box and make the kiss. Setting him back down, she bent to straighten his head square.

"I'm big enough," Hannah announced, as she reached up on tiptoe, barely touching the box and kissing her fingers. Thomas looked enviously at his older sister, which prompted her to repeat the ritual a second time for emphasis.

"Enough, Hannah," her mother responded, making her own sign of respect. "Let's get on the way."

Neighbors were streaming by on the road, everyone heading excitedly toward the village well. For a few minutes they were all kept busy greeting friends and exchanging the news of the day, and no one missed Thomas, who had knelt to examine a fresh spider web beside the path. Luckily Hannah looked back and called to him.

"Where is he?" Ruth asked, alarmed at how quickly he had gotten away in the crowd.

"He's looking at a bug back there on the trail," Hannah answered a bit pompously.

"Thomas!" Ruth called. "Come right now!" But he didn't. "Jesse," she began, but Jesse was already handing off the baby to her as he backtracked for his prodigal.

"Son, what are you doing?" he asked with some impatience.

"I found a spider," Thomas explained. It made good sense to him.

"What spider?" Jesse asked, examining the empty web.

"This spider," Thomas answered, cautiously opening one corner of his crumpled napkin so the cowering critter would not escape. "For the rabbi," Thomas explained seriously. "He needs a spider."

Jonas and his family went by just then, entertained by the snatches of conversation they could overhear. "Generous kid you've got there, Jesse," Jonas teased as he passed.

"Yes. Gets it from his mother," Jesse countered, embarrassed. "Come on, Son, you're holding the family up.

And put that spider back on his web. That's not a good gift for the rabbi. We'll find something else."

Thomas pouted, but obeyed, carefully shaking the spider out of the napkin, then running to catch up with his mother.

"What was that all about?" Ruth asked her husband, as they regrouped.

"Just the usual three-year-old distractions," Jesse answered, shaking his head. "He's still looking for a gift for the rabbi."

"Oh, we promised him, didn't we?" Ruth remembered.

"No, *you* promised him," Jesse corrected, taking David back. "This kid is getting heavy."

"Mama, will the rabbi like children?" Hannah asked.

"Why, Hannah, I certainly think so," Ruth answered with some surprise. The doubt had never entered her mind. "I have heard that he healed children—several of them. Yes," she said more confidently, "the rabbi surely will like children."

"Will he like my handkerchief?" she persisted. Ruth was getting the idea now. Hannah was a little fearful of what this visiting teacher would be like.

"Yes, Dear, he will think the handkerchief a fine gift," she assured her daughter.

"What will the rabbi do to us?" came next.

"He will just touch you, and say a blessing for you— that's all," Ruth explained. "You don't need to worry about it, Hannah. Papa and I would not take you unless he was a good man. This Jesus is a good man."

"But," Hannah persisted, "what if he is too busy to see us?"

"He'll see us, Baby," Ruth answered patiently. "We may have to wait our turn, but in time he will get around to us."

"Thomas, hurry!" Hannah called to her brother who had gone off the path to examine the ground more closely. "Mama, Thomas stopped again," she tattled with sibling joy.

"Thomas, come on now," Ruth called, but he didn't. Not amused, Ruth started back to get her son.

"Look, Mama," Thomas said with wonder, holding up a precious gem for her to inspect. "Jesus would like this pretty rock."

Ruth examined the rock carefully, trying to see it with three-year-old eyes. "It *is* a pretty rock, dear. I think it would make a lovely gift. Now, let's hurry, or he may be gone."

Thomas jumped happily back onto the path behind his mother's white skirt. He couldn't wait to get to the well and see the rabbi now. He had a wonderful treasure to share.

Behind the Scene
A Study of Matthew 19:13–15 and 18:1–11

Where is Beth Nimrah?

Jesus and his band had left Galilee and were en route to Jerusalem, where he would meet with crucifixion and death. They would not see Galilee again until after his Resurrection. The subject of his death had been introduced again and again, and–although they were deep in denial–the Disciples were aware that bad times might lie ahead.

Traveling south on the road east of the Jordan River, Jesus passed through the villages of Peraea in "the region of Judea (on) the other side of the Jordan." (Matthew 19:1–2) Few of these villages have names we recognize. Beth Nimrah was on the road, and one of the places Jesus would have walked by. Choosing it for our story was a probability, not a fact. We do know that the story happened while Jesus was in Peraea, moving toward Jericho and then Jerusalem.

Fame preceded him. Everywhere he had shown kindness to the people, providing miracles of healing when nothing else could help. Crowds followed and crowds gathered everywhere he went. These throngs were unusually varied. Besides Jesus, his men, and the women who often joined them on mission, there were the religious leaders of every town, always looking to set a trap that would discredit him and diminish his popularity. In the verses just before our story they accosted him for answers about divorce. Rubbing shoulders with the leaders were upper crust folks like the man we commonly call "the rich young ruler," and the prosperous tax collector, Zacchaeus. (Compare Luke's version in chapters 18 and 19.) Standing, crawling and lying at his feet, always there were the sick. (See Matthew 19:2.)

But the bulk of the crowd was simply made of folks–some believing, and some doubting. At this stop in Peraea, young families and grandparents grasped at the opportunity to bring small children for a blessing.

Most probably did not realize that they were catching Jesus as he struggled to keep his balance between friends and foes, life and death, on that day.

Blessing children was a usual thing for young Jewish parents. Especially around the first birthday, we are told, they sought out rabbis to bless their infants. Parenting is such an awesome responsibility, almost all parents covet the help of God in their task. Even in our world we seek out infant dedications—which are probably better called "parent dedications." As toddlers grow, we thoughtfully surround them with persons who will be positive role models. Doctors, preschool teachers, pastors, sitters, godparents, coaches—carefully we screen all these in an effort to fill our children's lives with attitudes and skills that can be emulated. Jesus was such a person, and his blessing would be a good omen for the little ones of Beth Nimrah, and the villages around.

Touch Point

Where does your life's path intersect with children? Almost certainly you are a parent, a teacher, a grandmother, an aunt, or a neighbor. Do you take time to bring your little ones before Jesus, asking for his blessing each day? Praying for children must be a continual discipline. Scripture tells us their angels "always see the face of the Father." How encouraging to know our prayers join with the forces of heaven for their health and protection! We must also pray for their

continuing growth and nurture in the things of the Lord. Then, we must keep our relationships with them vital so that God can use us in the answering of those very prayers.

Nurture Children in the Lord: Matthew 19:13–14

Aren't you glad this story was included for us? It has to be one of the gentlest, kindest, most heart-warming of all the Gospel accounts. Stop now and read the Matthew 19 verses to bring the poignant facts clear in your memory. *"Let the little children come to me, and do not hinder them."* What a command to us all!

We tend to frown at the Disciples for trying to hold back the surging crowd, but we must remember the tension of the day. Opposition was building, and their thoughts were toward protecting their beloved Master—and we might have done the very same in their sandals. Jesus' days were long and stressful. They had walked many miles, and had many more to go. But, in an unusual response, Mark tells us, Jesus spoke with indignation to these close associates (Mark 10:14) turning their own rebuke around on them. Children, we see, are more of a priority with Jesus than the Disciples had realized.

Children are priority with the Heavenly Father, also. Just days before, when the group was still in Capernaum, and while teaching on another subject, Jesus had occasion to tell the Disciples that in heaven the guardian angels of children have free and direct access to God at all times! (Search Matthew 18:10–11.) An astounding truth in our day, when children are subject to abuse, malnutrition, abortion, forced labor and other such atrocities.

This places in highest status those who nurture children in any significant way. *"Let the little children come"* to Jesus first, give them front row in all the workings of home, church and society. Take them on your laps and in your arms, as Jesus did (see Mark 10:16) and nurture them in the things of God. *"For of such is the kingdom of heaven."*

Did you enjoy the scene in the story when the father taught his infant son to touch and revere the Mezuzah—the box containing the Shema from the Law—which was affixed to every devout Jew's front doorpost? Parents are always and ever the primary teachers of spiritual things. God made it so in Deuteronomy 6:4–8. Mothers sing "Jesus Loves Me" as they rock their infants to sleep. Fathers join children for bedtime prayers. Family conversation respects and refers to Bible thoughts day and night. Mealtimes are begun by asking blessings. Parents make Bible teaching and worship a priority in every Sunday's routine. God wants it to be so.

Church and society are right to join hands with parents to see to the well-being of every child. Children are the unwitting victims of adult lives gone awry. They must be rescued from results for which they bear no blame—even if it costs us dearly. Every child must have a chance. They own the kingdom!

Touch Point

Perhaps you, like myself, feel frustration at the plight of children worldwide. On the television we see children in the Third World dying of starvation and AIDS. We know the resources exist to radically change those situations, but people and politics are blocking the way. We have no power over the problem, so we sometimes quash it with a squeeze of the remote control.

Ask God what steps you can take to become part of the saving of children. Easy answers run to contributing to reliable mission and rescue causes. Harder solutions involve ministries to children in your neighborhood. We cannot cure the world. We cannot rescue them all. But we can take one or two into our arms and our hearts and bless them.

Be Like Children in Humility: Mark 10:15

We skip to Mark's and Luke's accounts to get the complete words of Jesus here. Not only do children own the kingdom, adults may not enter unless they can assume an important childlike quality. Arrogance never enters the Kingdom of God—only humility walks through the door. We must know we are lost before we can be saved. We must drop our boot-strap efforts and embrace God's free gift of grace. We must *"sell our goods"* and come in empty-handed. Salvation is the work of God and not of us. Children are OK with that.

Prideful adults have a problem with it. As Dr. Herschel Hobbs pointed out, adults look at the simple truths of the Gospel, and think we must help children rise to a level of adult understanding so *they* can enter the Kingdom. Actually, we should be humbling ourselves and becoming like children, so *we* can enter.

That "other topic" Jesus was teaching on in Capernaum had to do with which of the Disciples would hold the highest position in the new Kingdom. (See Matthew 18:1–4.) We will look at that struggle up close in the next chapter, but only stop here to point up how adults continually jockey to be on top. In every aspect of life we erect ladders to climb. Beauty pageants, sporting events, business ventures, house sizes, church buildings—everything, especially in America—has to be in the category of biggest, newest, prettiest and fastest. Even in church life we see power funnels churning at the edge of every storm cloud. How disappointing that must be to the Savior who left heavenly realms to become the infant of a homeless couple, and made his first bed on straw in a feed trough. Any greatness about us comes from our personhood—the image of God within us–not in our position or possessions. We must cultivate childlike humility, and not with an eye to future reward.

Touch Point

It's time to check our "Childlikeness" gauge. If we find ourselves caught in the ladder-climbing mentality—focused on success or products—we need to adjust our R.P.M.

(Reaching People Modes). We can do that by taking an hour out to sit near a children's playground. (If we were braver, we would sit in a children's hospital.) Living children have a way of resetting our priorities from upward mobility to downward concern in just minutes.

Protect Children at All Costs: Matthew 18:5–9

Have you noticed that Matthew grouped some very important teachings about the family around this story of blessing the children? Chapters 18 and 19 speak about how we treat children, brothers, servants, marriage vows, and personal possessions. Children are affected by every one of those actions, as they watch the significant adults in their lives navigate the treacherous waters of family relationships and values. But the strongest warnings center on how we treat children.

Stop and reread Matthew 18:6. Then consider how many ways an adult can lead a child into sin. Different translations say, "causes…to sin," "leads astray," "cause stumbling," "offends." Few people are so calloused as to verbalize to a child how to do wrong. Fewer so evil and demented that they actually abuse and misuse a child physically. When we catch those, we put them in prison or in treatment. Most often what offends children is the selfish lifestyle that is demonstrated before them. Or the home ripped out from under them by broken promises. Or careless words that destroy and diminish the potential of such fragile lives. Children believe what adults tell them about themselves. They pattern after adults in their world, so the life badly lived, the words carelessly spoken, the values selfishly skewed—these are what make us guilty before God. Few seem to believe it.

Those who make every effort to live and speak in wholesome ways before children, then, are faced with living in a world where so many tramp them down. Our ministry becomes one of damage control, rebuilding, educating, legislating, praying and protecting. We would not be guilty of hurting children either by direct action, or by neglecting to be advocates for them. Pick your cause. Children must be protected by adults—we are all they have.

Touch Point

Rule out perfection. None of us is able to live around children without making grievous errors. Our guideline must be that we live in love and constructive goodwill towards the children of our world. Love will constrain us to reach out in some active way.

Do you know someone who has given his or her life to the nurturing of children in Jesus' name? Today would be a good day to drop a note of thanks and encouragement —and perhaps offer to get involved in some way. What better crusade? When we place ourselves beside/under/in front of a child, we are in the company of angels, in the Spirit of Jesus, and within the Law of God. Bring on the children!

Chapter 12

Ambitious

Salome, Mother of James and John
(Matthew 20:20–28 and 18:1–6)

Trees were silhouetted against the evening sky when Salome stepped outside the inn to catch a few quiet moments. A gentle breeze sent wisps of smoke and smells of strange foods her way. Travelers from Asia and a merchant caravan from Egypt were in the courtyard that evening, cooking their fare around the open fire. Animals tethered in stalls and in the open yard added to the aura of the night.

Looking for a quiet corner in which to collect herself after the long day, Salome walked a few steps to the little almond tree where James had tied their faithful mule. The inn was very busy tonight. She found a little comfort—a little feel of home—just in rubbing Jonah's familiar forehead and nose with her palm. She and

Zebedee had raised him from a colt, and he was like a member of the family. The mule snorted softly, tossing his head in protest of the strange surroundings.

The door squeaked and Joanna came out, munching a last piece of sweet bread. She joined her friend by the almond tree. "Want company?"

"Sure," Salome smiled. "You're limping again this evening, Joanna. The walk was hard on your sore ankle, I think. You really needed another day or two to rest it before traveling."

"I know," Joanna agreed, "but I couldn't ask the group to wait on me. And it helped to ride Jonah part of the day. Thank you for that." She gave her last bite to the nervous mule who munched it down, while she slowly surveyed the yard. "It's not very restful here tonight, is it?" she observed, wiping her hand on her wrinkled dress.

"No. I really dislike inns," Salome complained, "but this Jericho area is certainly too dangerous for camping out. Especially with no moon tonight. Even with as many of us as are traveling together, one can never tell."

"I think it's a toss-up which bandits we risk on—the highway robbers or the innkeepers," Joanna responded facetiously. "The world doesn't seem safe anywhere now."

"As many Roman troops as we saw on the road today, one would think travel would be more pleasant." Salome adjusted her veil as she spoke. "So much for the 'Roman Peace' we hear about!"

"Cuza says it works fine as long as there is a Roman soldier in sight." They smiled with eyebrows raised at the sad reality. Children ran past on an errand to draw a skin of water from the inn well. Across the court a small huddle of merchants pursued a dice game by light of a flare. "Life goes on—even here," Joanna mused absently, and they both sat down on a split rail near the tree.

"Tomorrow we'll see Jerusalem," Salome said. "And I wonder what will happen there."

"To Jesus?" asked Joanna.

"And to all of us," Salome responded. "James and John seem to think the crowds may overrule the Council, and sweep Jesus into power, and if that happens—the kingdom will officially begin."

"I guess we are all hoping for that," Joanna ventured. "But I'm not sure he is ready for it. I mean, a kingdom is a very big thing, and Jesus hasn't even begun to get organized for it. No positions, no appointments—only a wonderful way to live life. Surely he is going to set up some kind of structure, and name some of the men to positions before he makes a move like that. Even he cannot govern Israel alone! Look at all the people who work with Cuza in Herod's service."

Salome nodded agreement. "I've been thinking that, too. I'm afraid he will name Peter as his top officer, and that worries me."

"Why is that?" Joanna looked surprised.

"He's a good man, but so..." Salome was at a loss for words.

"So impetuous?" her friend offered.

"Yes—impetuous—and a bit dominant," Salome agreed, choosing her words carefully, and keeping an eye on the door of the men's hostel. "I'm not sure how that would work with the others—like Judas, who seems to see himself as the smartest one of the group."

"Or Matthew, who is so experienced? Or Simon, who is more political and aggressive?" Joanna's voice was low and confidential, and her thoughts paralleled Salome's well. "Judas I don't trust at all. I guess because my Cuza is a financial officer I see little things; but I think Judas may be a bit untrustworthy with the purse."

"Well," Salome admitted, "James has wondered about that, too."

"Personally," Joanna continued, "my choice for the highest place would go to your James. I think he is a very strong person—and quite wise. I could follow him. And I could follow Peter—but not Judas or Simon. And I don't know about Matthew." Joanna waited as the inn-keeper's wife and daughter passed by, bringing kindling and kitchen trash for the fire, then spoke again. "Don't you think Jesus has already picked out Peter, James and John as his most trusted? Actually, I thought he might have already appointed those three secretly—like when he took them up on the mountain."

"No," Salome paused thoughtfully, "he hasn't. But my James and John would both be good," she agreed. "Not just because I am their mother, but because they are good to the core, like their father. Zebedee has raised them well. They know how to work hard, and they can get along with people well. And, besides that, they are men of strong conviction. And nobody loves Jesus more than my John."

"John is a dear man, Salome. You have raised two good sons. And then there is the family thing," Joanna mused. "Aren't your boys cousins to Jesus? Many rulers prefer to have family in the positions closest to them."

"What would you think, Joanna…" Salome broke the sentence as the men's hostel door opened and James came out with a sleeping mat under his arm.

"Mama?" he called into the darkness.

"Over here, by Jonah," Salome answered.

"What are you girls doing out here under a tree in the dark?" James asked impishly. "Beelzebub will get you for sure! Don't you know it's time for bed?"

"Just talking girl talk," Joanna answered. "Are you not going to sleep inside tonight?"

"I think I'll just make my bed out here by Jonah. He smells better than that riff raff I'm traveling with," James quipped.

"It's so noisy out here, you may not get much sleep," Salome cautioned. "But I'm sure Jonah would like the company. He's a little edgy with all these strange people and animals around. He's used to his own stall, and a little privacy."

"Aren't we all?" James laughed. "Well, if I stay out here with him, I know he'll be here in the morning," he said under his breath. Salome saw him nod toward a group of camel drovers loitering across the yard. "Lots of folks would be glad to pick up a free mule for the road. So—" James eyed the two women knowingly—"tell me what you have to talk about that is so important it keeps you up past bedtime."

Salome could never keep secrets from this oldest son. From his youngest days they had shared most everything on their hearts. "We were just wondering about Jesus setting up his kingdom," she answered.

"Mama, we just have to wait on his time," James answered a little sternly. "We aren't in charge of that." He was fumbling in his duffle for some oats for the mule.

"I know, I know," Salome conceded, "but the time could be near, and he doesn't seem to be making some of the decisions he needs to make."

"Like?" James began, scooping two handfuls of oats into Jonah's pan. He turned to eye Salome. "Mama, are you back on the thing about John and me? Because, if you are, I want you to drop it. It's going to cause trouble in the group. Just let Jesus do it his way."

Salome looked down at the ground like a child caught in the cookie jar.

"I agree with her, James," Joanna chanced cautiously. "Maybe if we just prompted him a little it would help him decide what he is going to do."

James squatted down to look at the women on eye level. "I think Jesus probably knows what he wants to do. But—I don't know—maybe we could just—I don't know." Obviously the thought would not pass muster. "Let's just go to bed," he said, standing. "Tomorrow will be another long day." Kissing his mother, he walked around behind the mule and spread out his mat.

Salome and Joanna waited for him to settle down, and then continued in lowered voices. "You were going to ask me something, Salome. What was it?"

"I've forgotten," Salome hedged.

"About James and John being top leaders, I think."

"Oh!" Salome caught the gist of her previous thought. "I was going to ask, what do you think about James and John letting Jesus know they are willing to pay the price to be his right and left hand men in the new kingdom? Then, that still leaves him free to decide things as he will."

Late arrivers were banging on the inn's heavy gate as she tried to speak. It turned out to be a group of Roman soldiers with a couple of local conscripts in tow. Over shouts of the soldiers and insults from the unwilling load-bearers, further conversation was impossible. Joanna and Salome, watching the commotion with some fear, were startled to find James standing behind them protectively. It was not popular with the Jews to be forced to walk with the soldiers and carry their packs, and both those who saw and those who carried responded resentfully. It was another down side of the "Roman Peace."

"Mother, I want you ladies to go inside now," James insisted. "This is no place for you to be."

"I don't want you out here alone either, Son," Salome countered. "Go and get your brother and Peter and the three of you stay together. It will be safer."

"I'll get Simon and Thomas—they're scrapier than John. Now, inside you two!" And he walked them to the door.

"Well, we certainly do *need* another kingdom," Joanna whispered, as they found their beds beside the other women on the inn's straw floor. Outside, the courtyard seemed to slowly be settling down. Inside, Salome was still churning with indecision. Should she encourage James and John to speak up for their futures before the decisions were final? She fell into an uncomfortable sleep with the question unsettled.

Behind the Scene
A Study of Matthew 20:20–28 and 18:1–6

The Continuing Saga of Ambition: Matthew 18:1–6

Competition had been building for weeks within the disciple band. Before the group left Galilee Jesus had addressed it. Possibly it had surfaced about six months earlier, following the event we call the Transfiguration, found in Matthew 17. You remember at that time Jesus had singled out Peter, James and John to climb the mountain with him, and experience an unusual meeting with God. Why he chose to take only three is unknown to us, but the others were left to stand guard and protect his privacy at the foot of the mountain trail.

Several times Jesus elevated these same three Disciples over the others. When Jairus's daughter was healed (Mark 5:37) only these three were allowed to go with Jesus and the girl's parents to witness her raising. At the Transfiguration, only these three were allowed to be in the presence of Moses and Elijah, and to see Jesus' glory and hear the Voice of God. Later, in Gethsemane on the night he was betrayed and arrested, these same three would be invited to keep closer watch and pray for him in that darkest hour. Jesus seemed to have some purpose for taking Peter, James and John a step beyond the others in spiritual training. Very likely these were not the only incidents—just the three known to us. As the group traveled, lived and worked together, the difference may have been quite obvious.

What had that special favor done to the unity of the disciple band? And why had Jesus enabled it? Those questions may not have answers we can be certain of, but we can look at how Jesus handled their ambition as it developed.

Following the Transfiguration, the Disciples began asking, "Who is going to hold positions of greatest authority in the new kingdom?" (See Matthew 18:1–6). Perhaps they were jockeying for position among themselves. Or perhaps they wondered if Jesus would meld his kingdom into the existing political/religious order, and retain some of the priests and ruling class already in power. Or, having seen that Moses and Elijah were still in the picture, possibly they wondered if some of the Old Ones would be returning when the kingdom officially came. And it was not just the "other nine" who were asking. Peter, James and John also wanted the situation clarified.

Jesus chose to confront the problem of ambition—the innate human desire to be "first-est, most-est and best-est" in our worlds. The "let's play King of the Mountain" urge. The unending struggle to elbow each other as we climb the imaginary ladder of life's success. And he did it with a startling object lesson—a child. Was it one of the disciple's children? Mark 9:33 reveals this earlier conversation happened in the house at Capernaum. Jesus stood the child before them and drew some telling parallels. Unless adults change their spirits, and become childlike in some critical ways, they not only will be assured of zero position in the kingdom, they will not even *enter* the kingdom.

You have the wrong paradigm, he was saying. You are looking for prestige in all the wrong places. You seek it in power—but seek it instead in submission. You lust for authority—but greatness is found in meekness and service. Care about the vulnerable, the helpless, the needy. Seek to protect and mentor them. Imitate their innocence and low estate. After what model were the Disciples patterning their kingdom fantacies? The Roman authorities? The Jewish puppet kings? The Council of priests in Jerusalem? "We aren't going to be like any of them," Jesus kept saying. But the Disciples didn't get it. It's hard to understand things that are outside the realm of personal experience.

Touch Point

Oh my, oh my! Can we see ourselves all over these pages? Church life is fraught with incidents of little people seeking power and control. It doesn't take long to identify which boards or committees of the congregation have the power, and watching folks maneuver to get on these can be a study in manipulation. Often one who works up to the "in charge" position over finances or personnel will remain ensconced there for years, enjoying her or his place of privilege (and sometimes holding back the spiritual progress of the church).

Similarly, there are certain classes and ministries that seem to be at the top of the stack pole. It is never difficult to find a leader for a well-attended ladies' Bible study, but the preschool group may be begging for help. Visibility, name recognition, applause—these are the earthly rewards of the Kingdom. Sometimes we totally lose sight of Paul's, "For me to live is Christ," and "I am crucified with Christ." We drink the cup of champagne more fully than the cup of suffering.

God, turn our thinking upside down!

The Problem that Wouldn't Die: Matthew 19: 23–30

But ambition just kept raising its venomous head. The next time we are told about it follows upon their experience with the affluent yuppie politician we call the "rich young ruler." (His story is in Matthew 19:16–22). This man had so much on the outside, but felt empty on the inside. He came asking, "What can I do to make my life count–now and afterward?" Again, Jesus' answer was startling. "Get rid of all your stuff, and come with me on a life of voluntary poverty, service, helping, preaching, sharing. Turn from things to people. *Step from the kingdom of getting to the kingdom of giving*" (author's informal paraphrase). But the young man couldn't do it—he couldn't let go of all that made him feel successful and powerful. So he went away sad.

The whole incident left the Disciples standing in the middle of the road feeling very confused. Jesus could have had a powerful ally in that young man's company, but he let him get away. The man could have brought them wealth, acceptance, status, class—if you will; but there he was, walking home slump-shouldered. "If he is not what you want–who then?" asked the group, astonished. And then it hit them! *He wouldn't leave all and follow you, but that is exactly what we have done! So, what's in it for us? What kind of perks and benefits come with this job anyway? Is it going to pay off to be a disciple? Will we be rich and powerful one day? Or are we chasing the wind?*

Patiently Jesus explained the fine print to them again. In the end—the world after time—there will be power, position, prestige and prosperity. It will be worth it. Just keep your eye on the goal. Then followed the parable (see Matthew 20:1–16) in which he illustrated how fair God is in his evaluation of those who work in his fields. And how unable we are to evaluate each other—or even ourselves—from the standpoint of faithfulness and service. Matthew 20:12 says it concisely. "We gave you more than a full day, and these Johnny-come-latelys barely broke a sweat. We should get more than they do." And the master reminded them, "It's my business to decide position and reward. It's your business to be faithful" (author's paraphrase).

Touch Point

There are so many rewards to serving Christ. Life has meaning when we give ourselves over to his Kingdom. We enjoy some of the finest friendships and associations available—not just among the rich. We see lives changed and perhaps have a small part in affecting some of that change. This is Christianity in America—the land of freedom where, in spite of our pagan culture, church and religion still enjoy some respect, status, and liberty.

But consider this paradox: The true rewards of the Kingdom come as byproducts, not as goals. Those who join the kingdom with the ulterior motives of status and gain may just, "gain the world but lose their souls." It is only by coming to serve selflessly, by "taking up our crosses," being willing to "lose ourselves," that disciples enter into reward—and not primarily in this realm, but in the life to come.

Now is a good time to reread the familiar Beatitudes of Matthew 5:1–12 and see that the strange, unpopular life of the follower of Christ is promised no material reward here. The promised blessings are in our next

**life—in an eternal realm, "in the heavenlies."
Those who come seeking compensations in
this life are asking for Christmas in July.**

Then Mama Got into the Act: Matthew 20: 20–28

The pathos of this key story is revealed in contrast-
ing it to Matthew 20:17–19, the paragraph just before
it. It was time to climb the steep hill, leaving Jericho
in the Jordan Valley, for Jerusalem, on Mt. Zion. The
Crucifixion was only days away. Jesus could put it out
of his mind no longer. The burden of what lay ahead
was crushing him. He needed the understanding and
support of his men—all of them. This time he didn't
choose just three, but he called all Twelve aside for a
confidential meeting. Everyone else kept walking, but
Jesus and the Twelve stopped for one final *reality check*.
It cannot be plainer than Jesus' words in verse 18: "We
are going up to Jerusalem, and there I will be betrayed
to the religious leaders, condemned to die by crucifixion,
beaten and ridiculed, and killed. On the third day I will
come back to life." How deep was the sober hush that fell
on the group? It was as though Jesus was saying, "This
is going to be awful. If you want out, now is the time."
Nobody left—maybe because nobody really caught the
total seriousness of his words.

They had no more than rejoined the women and
the rest of their travel companions when Salome got
hold of her two strapping sons, James and John, and
came asking a secret favor of the Lord. (Mark 10:35 says
James and John did their own speaking here, but Mat-

thew credits it to Mama. Probably they were traveling on the family plan).

The question should be asked, "Which kingdom did Salome have in mind?" Did she mean the world after time, to which Jesus had referred in Matthew 19:28? Or did she mean the earthly kingdom she and the Disciples were still expecting would materialize when they got to the city? Or did she even distinguish between the two? Generally the later is assumed.

What astounds us is that Jesus was so patient with her/their question. With anguish of spirit barely under control, and every fiber of his being focused on staying the course and not running from the terrible fate ahead, Jesus took time to handle this intrusion with gentlemanly grace. Perhaps he was encouraged that, having just heard his predictions about the week to come, James and John were still so confident that he would eventually prevail. If he felt they had missed his whole point, he covered his disappointment well!

First he explained that the price of glory would be terrible and that they must suffer it with him. To reign with him they must be prepared to die with him. They were certain they could do so. Secondly, he told them that position and reward are not his department, but the Father's alone to assign. Jesus did not even admit to knowing God's plan for the organization of the Kingdom. He was focused on doing the work God had given him to do…one world at a time. This one was enough.

And then the free-for-all began. The other ten Disciples somehow learned what the secret conversation had been about, and they were indignant, angry, upset. *Why?* Because they were planning to ask for the same thing? Because James and John had gotten the jump on them and asked first? Because they smelled a family connection that excluded them unfairly? As Dr. Herschel Hobbs says, which of us dares to cast the first stone at them?* And the devil sat on the sidelines clapping with glee because at this most critical time, when the Disciples needed unity more than ever before, ambition had created division among them and stolen their sense of mission.

So, once more, Jesus sat them down and went over the plan. *"We are not like the others. We strive to serve, not control. We put ourselves last, not first—even, as you will see me do, to the point of dying for those who cause us pain."* Did they get it this time?

Touch Point

Jesus seized upon one last chance to explain the attitude he wanted in his leaders and followers. (We skip ahead in the story here.) It was just hours before his arrest. Everyone was enjoying the Passover meal when Jesus got up, left his host seat, took off his outer robe, and wrapped himself in a servant's towel. Kneeling on the floor in humility before each of his men, he began the menial task of washing their feet. They protested, but he insisted.

I have to show you, he seemed to say. *I have to set an example for you that you will not forget. No one is too good to serve. If I can do this to you in love, you can do this for each other.*

When we gather with believers, where is our towel? Often we are so hungry for friendship that we seek out someone to visit with us, turning the meeting or meal into a social occasion. Next time, stop! Look around for someone on the sidelines—someone who feels left out—and sit with her. Grab a mop and clean the floor. Go early and cook for the homeless. Volunteer to visit the sick. Pick up the trash that has been carelessly dropped on the parking lot or church lawn. Run transportation for those too elderly to drive. Ask what needs to be done and do it. Find every possible way to serve others. That's the kind of Kingdom Jesus wants, and the servant's heart he modeled for us.

*Herschel Hobbs, *An Exposition of the Four Gospels: Matthew*, Broadman Press, Nashville, TN 1965, Page 278.

Chapter 18

A Mite Generous

The Widow at the Treasury
(Mark 12:41–44)

Naomi lay quietly waiting for the dawn. She had wakened earlier than usual today—before the doves began gently cooing—and listened to the night sounds as she lay on her sleep mat. Swifts, crickets, frogs, an occasional cock calling to the setting moon—these familiar noises kept her company as she thought about the day ahead. Two houses away the dogs were barking, signaling that someone had begun the day. Her house seemed unusually dark, and both lamps were out, as Naomi shifted to her old knees and struggled to her feet. Breakfast would be quick today. With the oil all but gone it would not take long to bake the one cake she could eke out. *One good thing about being poor,* she mused, *is how simple life becomes when things grow scarce.*

Up now, she splashed her wrinkled face with some of yesterday's spring water and dried herself off on her skirt. Stains on the dress signaled that it was time to change to a clean one and take her wash to the creek, but soap is a luxury when oil is scarce. This dress would just have to do a while longer. Naomi cracked the window shutter slightly to let in some air and sunlight and met with the reason for morning gloom. Storm clouds had gathered over the city during the night, and the smell of a coming rain was heavy. *A good sign,* she thought, *because the gardens are struggling so against the severe drought.* Perhaps Jehovah would send the blessing of rain on them today. Then the cisterns would fill, and she could make fewer trips to the spring.

Days seemed to be repeating themselves now. Aching bones make for restless nights, and sleep is over before dawn for those as old as she. Rolling up her sleep mat, she swept the thatch into a neat pile in one corner of the floor. Dressing is easy for widows—no frills, no colors, no jewelry. Just the required grey/black of mourning day after day. It was as well, for her one gold necklace had long been sold for debts and taxes. Most mornings she busied herself just with surviving—or helping a few friends in more dire straits than she was. In good weather she gleaned winter wheat, or harvested new greens from the creek bank. These she shared with Sarai and Lois, who were too frail to gather for themselves now. Each trip to the spring sent her sharing the water with these same old friends. "Jehovah be praised that I have my eyesight and can still walk," she answered, when they protested her kindness. "It's good that one of us can go."

On afternoons when she was able, Naomi still made the walk to the temple for prayers. Her trademark in the neighborhood was the generous satchel that was always slung over her shoulder. She walked with her eyes to the ground, gathering kindling here and there for her cooking fires. And on occasion, as she passed Reuben's market, she received as alms a lamb bone or some over-ripe vegetables for her bag. Reuben's wife remembered kindly the days when Naomi and David had been regular customers, trading their garden fare and fresh milk for daily needs. But this was now the ninth Passover since David had succumbed to the cough, and Naomi was no longer able to raise the goods for barter. Whatever was given her in kindness she shared with others in need.

The morning passed still cloudy, but the rains never broke. In early afternoon she munched a gruel of crushed wheat in her doorway and watched the pilgrims pass on their way to the temple. Passover was now only three days away, and travelers streamed into the city, the lucky ones headed for homes of relatives. Lodging would be scarce throughout the week's end. A movement by the threshold caught her eye, and she smiled. "So there you are," she said to her little friend. "I missed you yesterday, and thought maybe a bird had you for breakfast. But you must have hidden well." The lizard cocked his head and remained still at the sound of her voice. He had long since learned that he was safe at Aunt Naomi's house. At times he even snuck in to spend the night, always startling her in the morning. Now as she watched him he snagged a flying bug with his lightning-quick tongue. "That's the way! Catch it wherever you can—just like me!" she teased.

It was almost time to begin the short trip to the temple. Walking to the shelf to get her satchel, Naomi's eyes fell on the little boat that sat beside her lamp. It was only the toy of a nine-year-old boy, but to her it was a precious work of art. The tattered sail hung limply, and she gently blew away the dust. It had been Benjamin's pride because he made it himself in his third year of school. How she needed that only son to care for her now! What a comfort he would be. But somehow Jehovah had needed to take him in his tenth year. David had never recovered from his grief, and somehow she felt it had hastened his death.

And so, Naomi was alone. Widows as old as she seldom returned to their own families. And all she had left in her old home town now was one cousin and his son, who probably would not have welcomed another mouth to feed. Then there was the matter of Sarai and Lois. Who would look after them? No, it was best to stay here, near David's nephew, and try to be as little trouble as possible.

Next to the toy boat was a small alabaster jar. Naomi picked it up, removed the lid, and searched its shallow depths with two fingers. Two tiny coins were her reward—all that was left after she had paid her temple tax. Looking at them she asked aloud, "Are you lonely in there—you two pitiful little coppers?" And, not knowing why, she tossed them into the bottom of her bag and left, closing the door behind her. *Maybe Reuben will sell me just a tad of oil for these lepta,* she thought. *Or maybe not.*

She was almost to the temple when raindrops began to pelt her veil and shoulders. Younger walkers were running for the porches, but Naomi knew it was best to take her time. Getting wet would be better than turning an ankle on slick pavestones. Soon enough she took cover under the arches of Solomon's Porch, where she had plenty of company. As she stood watching the merchants in the open area scramble to cover their wares against the rain, a slight tug pulled at her sleeve. Naomi turned to see her neighbor's daughter, Rebekah, beside her, almost as wet as she was. Naomi had known Rebekah since before she was born.

"It's terribly crowded today," Rebekah fussed. "All these holiday visitors, and everyone trying to stay out of the rain. Have you been here long?"

"Just got here," Naomi answered, smiling at her young friend. "How about you?"

"We came about an hour ago. We've been listening to the Nazarene—Jesus. He was teaching in the Women's Court until the rains came," Rebekah said. "It was really interesting."

"I've heard him before," Naomi told her. "What happened today?"

"A lot of arguing and confronting," said Rebekah, wiping her older friend's face gently with her veil. "You did get really doused, didn't you?"

"After all the dry days, the water actually feels refreshing," Naomi assured her. "I hope some of it catches in the cistern. What was the arguing about, and with whom?"

Rebekah's voice dropped to a whisper. "The leaders were angry. They were asking him a lot of tricky questions, like about paying the Roman taxes, and why he teaches a Resurrection."

"I hope Jesus put them in their place!" Naomi responded quietly into Rebekah's ear.

"He held his own more than well," Rebekah muffled her answer behind her hand. "He told them they were arrogant and dishonest, and said they took advantage of widows."

"And he is absolutely right," Naomi nodded. "I'm still smarting about Rabbi Aleph trying to get me to sign a paper to give him my house 'for the good of the temple.' Where would I live?"

"Oh, Auntie, when did *that* happen?" Rebekah was surprised and annoyed.

"Just last month!" Naomi replied with indignation. "As if I am about to die and leave it to him! I mean, I realize I have no heirs to claim it, but even so, rabbis are not supposed to take advantage in that way. The Law tells us that."

"Why, your house is all you have left, Auntie," Rebekah agreed. "How awful of him to come to you like that! If he had forged the papers, no judge around would have heard your case. I wish you had called Judah and me—we would have defended you."

"Don't worry about me, dear," Naomi assured her. "I don't have much to my name, but Jehovah is on my side. He has promised to protect the widows and orphans. But thank you for offering your help. Some days I feel very alone."

The horns had announced the hour for prayer, and both women were moving carefully across the wet courtyard and into the Court of Women. Through the open gates to the inner court Naomi could see the priests offering incense. Smells of sacrificial meat roasting and priest's bread baking wafted over the heads of the guests and made her hungry for a good meal, but she gave herself to prayer instead.

Prayers ended, and Naomi and Rebekah said their goodbyes and parted ways. A little drizzle caused Naomi to stay under the covered porches most of the way to the gate, a route that took her by the row of treasury boxes. Coins clanked noisily as worshipers dropped in few or many, depending on debt…or devotion…or the attention they hoped to gain. Naomi owed nothing. Her taxes were paid, and she had no income to tithe. But the memory of days when she and David could do more stirred in her heart. *The hardest part of poverty,* she complained silently to God, *is having nothing to give you in return for your blessings. Nothing for the children. Nothing for the temple.*

Easing toward the wall, Naomi leaned against it and took her satchel down from her shoulder. Inside she found and fingered her last two coins. *Can you use these?* she continued her wordless prayer. *There are only two, but two are better than one.* Slipping into a break in the line, she joined those walking past the boxes, coins in hand. Without looking up or betraying her intent, she gently slid the two small coins into one of the trumpets and continued on past. Perhaps no one would notice how small a gift she gave.

The rain had stopped for a while, and a patch of blue sky was breaking as she turned toward home. She passed the two blocks of fine homes, knowing by the smoke and aroma that inside they were preparing lavish Passover feasts for their families and guests. If she were younger she would offer her help to cook and serve, but the days of working on her feet for hours had passed with her last several birthdays. Across the street was Reuben's market, but having nothing with which to buy, she turned to detour by the creek bank. Perhaps some spring vegetables or early figs would keep hunger away tonight.

"Aunt Naomi," came a voice from behind her. "It's me, Joshua."

She knew him as Judah's older brother and stopped to let him catch up.

"Shalom, Auntie. I wanted to remind you I still have some winter wheat for you to glean. Are you able to make the walk?" he asked with genuine concern.

Naomi bowed in gratitude to the younger man. "Thank you, Joshua. Most days I can, yes."

"If the rains clear off, come tomorrow," he invited her. "If I don't see you, I'll send Simon with a basketful for you. We have to get it out of the field before it sours." And with a friendly pat he was on his way.

Naomi's heart was lighter for having felt his compassion. Her Benjamin would have been like that, had he lived to be full-grown. Passing next to a fig tree, she found half-a-dozen fruits nearly ripe enough to eat and picked them for her bag. They would be supper tonight, with enough to share!

Home again, Naomi found that a little rain had leaked onto her lamp table. She was mopping it up when she heard a knock. It was Esther, Rebekah's mother, from next door.

"Naomi, we want you to share our lamb stew this evening," Esther said, putting a small pot onto her hearth. "Goodness, girl, it's dark in this house," she complained.

"Oil is scarce," Naomi answered simply. "And thank you so much for the stew. I'll enjoy it for supper tonight. It will keep away the chill."

But Esther wasn't finished speaking. "And look, Naomi! I brought you these two widows' dresses and a very nice shawl," she said, spreading them over a chair. "They were my aunt's, but she has passed on, and I thought they would fit you perfectly. She was very near your size."

Naomi was too overcome to speak. "Jehovah is good," she said finally, her eyes shining. "And he cares for the fatherless and widows, as he promised he would."

Esther hugged her friend and started for the door. "Enjoy the stew, and—about the oil—we have extra. I'll send Little Judah over with a cruse before night. No need your being in the dark."

The door closed, leaving Naomi alone as before, but now…for a while at least…she was wrapped in the loving care of friends.

Behind the Scene
A Study of Mark 12:41–44

Finding Purpose in Aloneness

A frightening truth in every generation is this: The majority of women live out the end of their lives alone. With all the advances in medicine and science, with all our efforts to preserve the health of our menfolk, women, by a large margin, still outlive men. Not just husbands, but brothers, friends, and often even sons. It is an advantage that we neither like nor want. In the current struggle for equality, this is the goal we would most desire to achieve: to finish our lives together with those we love beside us to the end. Becoming a widow is a very real dread for many women.

For those who have experienced—or are currently engaged in—a lifelong marriage with a friend, it is difficult to imagine making the transition through grief to singleness. My mother was a widow almost thirty years, or more than one-third of her life. While that is longer than most, many women find themselves with a generous piece of life left over after marriage. When that happens, we have to come to grips with a very difficult dilemma. *How do we survive and build a purposeful second life when our partner and friend goes ahead of us?*

The widow in our story, scholars tell us, was (from the choice of words by which Luke described her) a pauper and alone. That left her quite vulnerable, subject to abuses by society and religion. Unable to pay for the basic necessities of life, unable to pay bribes to get justice in the courts, unable to buy medical help when needed, she would have been at the mercy of friends and neighbors. As her strength waned, her lifestyle probably deteriorated. Although The Law required Jews to treat orphans and widows fairly (see Exodus 22:22–24) a widow herself had little power to see that statute was enforced.

Yet in her search for meaning in life, this widow found humble ways to reach out to others. The treasury boxes were beyond the duty to tithe. They were freewill offerings for children of the needy, and for the work of the temple. She could have looked inward to her own need, but she chose to look outward to help others.

Touch Point

Have you been watching the widows in your church family as they rebuild their "life after life?" Which ones do you admire? What causes or ministries have they selected to benefit from their remaining strength and labors?

Wherever you now are in life—young adult, middle adult, senior, married woman or single—what goals would you set for your later phases of life? Never were Jesus' words more pointed to us than when he admonished, "But seek first his kingdom and his righteousness, and all these things will be given to you as well" (Matthew 6:33). The end time of life can be our finest hour!

In Search of Her Motive: Mark 12:41–44

The temple was packed to the walls with pilgrims that day, most in their holiday finery. Many brought sacrifices and offerings—all of them larger than the tiny gift of this woman. But among the throngs Jesus heard only two coins—the two lepta, which came to less than a quarter of a penny! Why did she give when she couldn't afford it and certainly did not have to?

Put into the larger context of this day spent by Jesus and his men at the temple, our widow draws some striking contrasts. Earlier a coalition of religious and political leaders had tried to trap Jesus with the now-famous question, "Do we have to pay taxes to Caesar?" (See this story in Mark 12:13–17.) Disguised in that query was the unspoken, *How can we keep more of our money in our own pockets?* Against their attempt to entangle our Lord in a hot financial issue comes this little woman with no agenda, just a desire to do something right and good for her God and her world.

Following on the heels of that political debate came Jesus' scathing discourse against the hypocritical motives of the religious leaders. (Read this in Mark 12:38–40, or an even stronger account in Matthew 23, entire chapter.) He exposed the temple leaders for their desire to wear pretentious robes with fancy borders, to be called by titles of honor and status, to sit in the most prestigious seats at dinner and events, and to pray gaudy prayers in public places. Even worse, he accused them of bilking widows out of their estates in the name of religion. Jesus' life was drawing to an end, and he had little to lose. No longer avoiding these powerful moguls of established Judaism, he cut loose with the ugly truth. It was a stinging frontal attack—and the crowds loved it! (See verse 37.) Against this "What's-In-It-For-Me?" religion comes one fragile lady with a simple desire—to give what she could to someone else.

As worshipers came into the temple area they encountered the open Court of the Gentiles, filled with merchants, greedy to make a healthy profit from the holiday crowd. This was the very area Jesus had "cleansed" just the day or two before! No doubt his demonstration was short-lived. Against their determined, often dishonest, certainly nonreligious purposes, comes this unspoiled soul wanting only to enter into the hour of prayer.

Allow one more comparison: Our widow was lost in a crowd of givers, most of whom were giving "pocket change," or easy money as an offering. Probably none of them went home to an empty pantry and a dried-up oil lamp that night. Theirs were the "over and above" gifts of the comfortable and wealthy. Some of them tossed them ostentatiously into the boxes so they would clank loudly and turn heads. Men noticed, but God looked away. Against this flashy show comes a destitute widow, ashamed that she has so little to give, hoping no one will notice. And God smiled.

Touch Point

Rethink the motives we found in the widow who gave all she had.

- **She wanted to meet some needs in her world.**
- **She wanted to give to others, and not focus on herself.**
- **She desired a time of genuine prayer and worship in God's house.**
- **She gave sacrificially, beyond her means, to do her part.**

Play those thoughts against your own motives for giving to God's work. "Search me, O God," to know that in my giving I carry no desire to be seen and recognized, no hope for reward and glory, no sense of drudgery or duty, no scheme to protect my own comfort at the expense of others.

How Could She Let Go?

Once long ago we knew a widow who simply *had to give*. Her home was a modest house, where she was raising a teenage daughter and had custodianship of a mentally handicapped adult brother. She lived by her garden, her sparse welfare check, and the occasional kindnesses of friends and family. Yet, every time a gift-giving occasion arrived, she was ready. When the Christmas offering for missions was announced, she was prepared. For weeks she had been saving small coins, and here would come her offering envelope, stuffed and taped shut, with money she could not spare, $1.75, $2.25, or some such humble amount.

She loved her pastor and his family—especially our little boy. Each Christmas she insisted on giving a gift to each of us. One year my gift was her autographed, first-edition printing of a little book by Dr. Charles Allen, which I treasure to this day. For the baby, a colorful little pillow with bells sewed to the corners. She made it of sewing scraps and stuffed it by taking the fill from a pillow of her own. He got finer gifts that year, but none more thoughtful or loving. I protested, "But you shouldn't," and she responded, "But I want to give, too!"

Much later in our lives we knew a single mother who was raising her small sons without benefit of child support. In addition, she was paying off bad debts left her by an ex-husband. She worked three jobs: one full-time, and two part-time. Our church was planning a new building, and we were all challenged to make sacrificial commitments. At the fundraising dinner, many testimonies were given along the lines of, "Our family planned to buy a new car, but we are going to put it off for two years and give those payments each month to the building fund." "Our family was planning to put in a swimming pool, but we have decided to give that amount to the church." "We plan to double our tithe for the next three years," and so on. But the single mom was already giving more than a tithe, and working well over sixty hours a week.

When her pledge came in it was this. "I'm taking on an Avon route, and everything I can earn for the next three years will go to the building fund." It made all our "sacrifices" look like icing on the cake, which is just about what they were. Again, I protested, "But you are already giving more than a tithe, plus hours of your time. God understands." And she responded, "But I want to do something for the Lord in this, too!" She gave more than all of us.

How could the widow do it? Give her last coins, not knowing what lay ahead? It's a *heart* thing. *She was a giver at heart.* She didn't have to see the answers, but she *had* to give! Some of us can't even come within shouting distance of understanding that. It contains a large measure of faith that God will keep his promises and provide for our basic needs. It has an element of recklessness in it, a generous scoop of sacrifice, and a whopping portion of thanksgiving.

How Can We Help?

Jesus loved widows and showed unusual concern for them, an emphasis Luke magnified for us in his Gospel. Luke alone tells us of Anna, the widowed prophetess who comforted the baby and his parents at his dedication (see the story in Luke 2:36–38). Luke also tells the story of Jesus' raising the only son of the widow at Nain (see Luke 7:11–17). He included two teachings that featured widows: the parable of continued prayer (Luke 18:1–8) and the case of the widow in the Resurrection (Luke 20:27–36). Looking at this we are not really surprised, because Jesus said at the outset that he had come to help the poor and oppressed and outcast. Many think that, by this point in his life, Jesus' own mother was a widow. This could help account for his giving her into the care of John, his most trusted friend, as he was dying on the Cross (John 19:25–27).

We took the liberty in "Naomi's" story at the first part of this chapter to go a further step, showing how God may have honored her faith by providing for her needs. Remember who helped God in that cause? Her neighbors made provision, and shared with her. Esther paid attention to her needs and met them without waiting to be asked. Any sensitive Christian can be the one to make the life of an elderly person more comfortable and joyful. The words of James challenge us strongly here. "Religion that God our Father accepts as pure and faultless is this: to look after orphans and widows in their distress and to keep oneself from being polluted by the world" (James 1:27). If time doesn't permit us to see and act on the needs of the vulnerable persons about us, something needs to move out of our lives so there will be room for this. What counts with God must also count with us.

Touch Point

The crux of the matter for us may be right here. With so great a percentage of our population now elderly and life getting longer each decade, ministering to older persons must become part of our daily routine.

We have mothers, aunts, neighbors, saints of the congregation, and the many forgotten ones who need to feel valued and cared for in their later years. Some portion of our time must be left available to God so that we can be his angels of mercy, sent to fulfill his promises to those who are no longer able to work, drive, mow their lawns, see to read, or enter into the worship and social activities of life by themselves.

"Lose your life—and you will find it!"

There is such a delicate, important, line between enabling an older person to live a fulfilled and independent life for a while longer and taking over her right to self-determination. God give us the wisdom and sensitivity to see the difference.

Part 4

WOMEN TOUCHED BY JESUS' DEATH AND RESURRECTION

Chapter 14

Courage to Speak Out

Joanna, Wife of Herod's Steward, and Pilate's Wife
(Matthew 27:11–26)

"Joanna, you need to get started before it gets any later." Salome was putting the last few dirty cups onto a tray as she spoke. "The Marys and I can finish this up now, and we will be staying downstairs tonight, but you have the walk to the palace ahead of you, and it is getting quite late. I'm almost afraid for you to go alone."

Joanna scraped two last bowls of sweet fruits and bitter herbs onto a nearly empty meat platter, stacking the remaining dishes to be washed. "Can't thirteen men make a mess, though?" she asked, looking up. "I know I need to get to the palace, Salome, but I hate to leave you with all the work. Cuza is probably frantic now with all the extra guests. Herod and Herodias came with him from Galilee last Sabbath. You know how she loves a feast—even if she isn't much of a God-fearer. And two days ago Pilate and Claudia arrived from Caesarea with the usual pomp and fuss. I guess he has to come to town during weeks like this to try and keep the peace. Everyone prefers staying at Herod's mansion because it is so plush and spacious. Anyway, Cuza probably needs me and wonders why I am out so late."

"He may be out of his mind with worry," Mary Clopas sympathized. "Salome is right, she and I can finish up, and we need to get Jesus' mother settled for bed. Are you afraid to walk through the Upper City by yourself?"

"*I* certainly would be!" exclaimed Salome.

"I think I can probably find one of Herod's guards in the vicinity of Caiaphas' house, and he will accompany me," Joanna responded. "They know me…and would happily do any favor to stay on Cuza's good side."

"Now that I think about it," Salome persisted, "maybe you should just stay here for the night, then go home in the early morn…—what was *that!?*"

All four stopped to listen to the night sounds below. "Probably a dog looking for garbage," Joanna guessed.

"It's too early for the men to come back. Anyway, I think they will sleep out in the cool of the garden tonight when their prayers are over," the older Mary offered. "I don't expect them back until morning myself."

Footsteps sounded on the outer stairs, and four pairs of eyes went to the door. Thomas was first in, followed by James and Andrew—all of them ashen with fear. Thomas put a finger to his lips in warning.

When the three were in and the door bolted shut behind them, James motioned the women to come close. "Jesus has been arrested," he whispered tensely. "We are all in danger. Put out the lights and stay very quiet. We may have been followed."

"Arrested by whom?" Salome demanded hoarsely, as Joanna began snuffing lamps.

"By Caiaphas's men—the temple guard," James responded. Jesus' mother sank onto a couch; the younger Mary caught her and held her close, rocking her back and forth as she sobbed silently into her friend's breast.

"But the Roman guard was with them," Thomas added, "so Pilate is in on it. Judas betrayed us, the lying bastard! I should have killed him weeks ago!"

"Where did this all happen?" asked Joanna. "Are you certain the Romans are involved? They don't usually care about religious matters."

Andrew spoke softly, reaching to pat Jesus' mother gently, as he explained. "Caiaphas brought them on—for authority, I guess. It doesn't bode well."

"Fat thief that he is!" Thomas blurted. "Fat on our temple taxes and Roman bribes!"

"Where are the others?" the older Mary asked tearfully. "Peter? John? Phillip?"

"John followed the soldiers that took Jesus. John knows some of the temple staff, and he thought he might be able to intervene. But Peter, well…" Andrew's voice trailed off, not knowing how much to reveal to the women.

"What about Peter?" Salome pressed as James signaled her to lower her voice. "Did something happen to him?"

"Not exactly," Andrew hedged.

"We may as well tell you," James conceded. "Peter drew a sword in all the confusion at Gethsemane and wounded Caiaphas' servant. He'd be wise not to show his face right now."

"Oh, Peter!" the older Mary wailed softly. "He wanted to help, but he is so clumsy."

"As for the others," Thomas continued, "I guess we don't know. If they aren't here, they may have headed back to Bethany or somewhere outside the city for safety. Jesus asked the soldiers to let us all go."

"I guess we *are* all in danger," Salome agreed. "And for no more reason than that we loved him and believed in him. I do hope John can prevail with them. What do you think will happen next? Is there a chance they will let Jesus go? It isn't even lawful for them to arrest and try someone during the Passover."

"I think…" James began, but stopped to look at Jesus' mother. "Aunt Mary, I am so sorry, but the news is not good. We think they will trump up a charge and then take him to Pilate tomorrow for sentencing. Caiaphas has little power of his own, and he has involved the Romans for a reason. We think he will go for the worst punishment."

"You mean, the death sentence?" asked the younger Mary in unbelief. "Surely not! Not someone as good as our Jesus! The people won't let that happen! He has done too many miracles for them, and they love him too much!"

Joanna moved to the troubled mother's side and knelt to see her face. "We won't let that happen to your son, Mary! We will find some way to stop this insanity before it gets to that point. We will pray, and God will show us something to do."

Mary reached out, clinging to her hand, grasping for hope. "Yes, we must pray," she echoed. "Oh, Father, protect my son. Protect my Jesus."

"We may not be able to stop them, Joanna," Thomas countered quietly.

Everyone turned, stunned by his bleak words. "Don't say that, Thomas," Salome scolded. "Surely God will stop them."

"No," Thomas insisted. "He may not. This is exactly what Jesus has been saying to us: 'I am going away…the Son of Man will be scourged and handed over to the chief priests and Romans, and they will crucify him.' We haven't been listening, because we didn't want to hear it. But I think we may be heading into the most tragic days of our lives."

"Oh, God! No! *No!*"Joanna insisted. "I can't sit still for this. I know Pilate's wife, Claudia. She is a Jewish sympathizer—and she has heard Jesus teach. We talked about it in the women's quarters the other day when she first arrived. I'll go to her and ask her to talk with Pilate and tell him not to agree to a death sentence. I think she may listen to me, and she is in position to speak out on his behalf."

"Yes, go!" Salome agreed quickly. "That's our best hope. James, go with her, son. She doesn't need to be on the streets alone in this second watch—especially now."

"I'll go with you, Joanna," the younger Mary volunteered. "I'll stand with you any way I can."

No, I need to go alone." Joanna gathered up her shawl and bag and started for the door as she spoke. "I am well-known, and it will not arouse suspicion for me to go to the palace at this hour. The rest of you would be in danger."

Thomas stepped in front of her and blocked her way. "James and I will walk with you, Joanna," he said firmly. "You cannot go out alone on the street tonight. We will follow you, staying in the shadows, and drop back when you reach the safety of the palace. No one will know we are there."

"But," she protested, "if you are caught...?"

"We won't be," Thomas assured her. "James and I know the safe alleys, and..."

Joanna nodded consent, and the three said their goodbyes quickly and left. Outside the darkness covered them like a veil. Though most people were sleeping, here and there someone was watching a fire, turning a lamb on the spit for tomorrow's dinner. An animal tied and awaiting the morning sacrifice bleated a loud protest as they passed. Joanna drew her shawl closer against the early morning chill.

Thomas chose the street that ran above the west side of Caiaphas's mansion. Lights there were blazing, and the three could see servants and guards watching at all the gates. As they passed, two of the council members arrived and entered quietly. "They must be having a meeting now, even though it is dark," James whispered.

"They probably can't get enough of those fat pigs out of their fancy beds at this hour to get a quorum!" Thomas shot back. "Meetings in the dark hours are not even legal—it's more of Caiaphas's treachery!"

"We must hurry!" Joanna cautioned.

Heavy footsteps ahead signaled a Roman night guard approaching. James pulled Joanna into a narrow passageway between two houses, accidentally stepping on a sleeping dog that limped away whimpering. The three crowded into a doorway as the brace of men passed by. When it was safe James signaled, and they stepped back onto the street, picking up their pace.

Turning west and then north, Thomas indicated a series of secluded alleys that brought them almost to Herod's imposing residence. All gates were barred, and Joanna led them around back. "Malachi will be on duty here, and he knows me. I can gain entrance by him," she whispered. "You both were so kind to come with me, but now you must not come any closer. Be careful going home. I will do my best to make contact with you tomorrow. Pray for me."

As she walked toward the back gate Thomas and James hunkered back into the night, watching guardedly. Joanna rang a small bell and didn't have long to wait. One of Herod's slaves approached, smiling when he saw her. "Miss Joanna," he whispered, "what you doing out at this hour—and alone? Mr. Cuza will worry."

The gate hinge squeaked as she entered. "It's all right, Malachi," she assured him. "The guards brought me home. Is Cuza asleep yet?"

"Yes, Ma'am. He gone to bed just lately. Been so busy. Those ladies hard to please."

"Malachi, what time does Pilate's wife usually waken in the morning?" Joanna asked.

"Oh, she not early, Ma'am," he said, shaking his head emphatically. "Up late tonight. Pilate have visitors. Sent out soldiers. His lady upset and fussin'. Guards come back noisy. Nobody sleep alot. Late breakfast in the morning."

"Call me when Cuza gets up, please. I must talk with him about an important matter," she said, turning to go into the women's quarters. "Please don't forget to call me, Malachi—however early it may be."

"Oh, yes, Ma'am. I call Ma'am when the Master rises," the old Ethiopian assured her. And Joanna tiptoed in for a sleepless night.

Behind the Scene
A Study of Matthew 27:11–26

Making the Connection

On what farfetched line of evidence have we linked Joanna, the wife of Herod's household manager, and Pilate's wife?

We first meet Joanna in Luke 8:1–3, where she is identified as one of the women who traveled with Jesus and his men throughout Galilee, caring for their needs and supporting them from private funds. She is called the wife of Cuza, Herod's household administrator. Herod Antipas, Tetrarch of the two provinces of Galilee and Peraea, had residences in both areas. Cuza and Joanna may have made his palace at Tiberius in Galilee their primary home. As steward, Cuza would have seen to all the matters of Herod's house, including the finances in one or both locations.

Jumping to Luke 24:10, we discover that Joanna was in Jerusalem at the time of Jesus' death. Since we know that Herod was also there (see Luke 23:6–7), it is very possible that Cuza had come to see to his affairs on the trip.

As for Pilate's wife, historians tell us her name was Claudia Procula, and that she and Pilate preferred to reside in Caesarea instead of Jerusalem. Pilate disdained the Jews and their rigid religious practices and had won their great disfavor by disrespecting their holy places in many ways. But on feast weeks he was obligated to be in the city to oversee peacekeeping efforts. Although Pilate's Jerusalem accommodations would ordinarily have been the military headquarters building called the Praetorium, when he brought his wife along, researchers tell us, they chose to stay in the more suitable surroundings of Herod's Palace. That mansion, which had been built in the Maccabean era, was claimed years earlier by Antipas' father, Herod the Great, and made into palatial quarters. Visiting dignitaries made it their *hotel of choice.*

Further inquiry into Claudia's background indicates that she was a religious woman who sympathized with the Jews. Some even claim she became a convert to Judaism, and later to Christianity. The Coptic (Egyptian

Christian) Church declared her a saint for her futile but brave efforts to try to stay the execution of the Lord. Did Joanna, wife of Cuza, influence her in that? We have to imagine she would have if she could have.

Touch Point

The words of Queen Esther and her godly Uncle Mordecai echo down to Joanna here: "Who knows but that you have come to royal position for such a time as this?" And, "I will go… and if I perish, I perish."

Every woman has to assume that she has been strategically placed in her world of influence for some special purpose of God. We do not always know at what time in our lives that *critical moment* of opportunity will come. It may not be as significant a crisis as Joanna's and Esther's were—an event on which history itself turns—but the occasion is ours to seize and rise to.

To Esther's words we could add those of Mary to Gabriel: "I am the Lord's servant. May it be to me as you have said." Be ready. We must remain ready for God's call.

A "Courage Hall of Fame"

In the story of Jesus' tragic arrest, trial, and Crucifixion (Matthew 26:36–75), we have an incredible string of courageous acts detailed.

Jesus, more than anyone, showed tremendous resolve in his Gethsemane decision to allow himself to be arrested, and enter into the ordeal ahead of him, for the purpose of redeeming the world to his Father. He could have disappeared over the mountain as his men lay sleeping through the hour of prayer, but he chose to stay and fulfill the plan of God for which he had been born into our world. Fully aware of the agony waiting him, he charged the arresting guards to release all his men; then stepped out boldly to face the inevitable *alone.*

Peter's clumsy attempt to defend his Lord against a large band of armed soldiers, with only a short sword, was an act of uncommon valor. And that he followed the disgraceful band on to the High Priest's house, knowing he would be identified, shows more incredible bravery. True, he disgraced himself in the denials that followed, but even they must be seen against the backdrop of his other acts of courage.

The List Continues: Matthew 27:27–65

Jesus himself, of course, continued to lead the list of heroes as he faced up to the three most powerful men in the city: Caiaphas, Pilate, and Herod, admitting to his divine mission, making no attempt to free himself from the awful death to come. He endured beatings, insults, and indignities throughout the endless and biased hearings. What an example he set for us all—even in death!

Mary, his mother, always amazes us with her tenacity and devotion. Can you see her making her way slowly up the hill of crucifixion, perhaps on the arm of her dear nephew, John, to stand by her accused son in this final, dreadful hour? With a broken heart full of love she stood beneath his Cross, seeking to give him strength, praying to the end for a miracle, watching helplessly as he died. And now we know why God chose her those many years before to be the mother of his precious son. On she stayed—through the death, burial, Resurrection—until his final victory at Pentecost. No coward, that Mary. A heroine of the faith. We will look at her closely again in our final chapter.

Next see **Joseph of Arimathaea,** and **Nicodemus,** both dissenting members of the condemning Council, the Sanhedrin. What kind of courage did it take for these men to identify themselves to their fellows as Christ's followers in his hour of greatest disgrace? And to go before Pilate, the hated Governor, to request his body for burial? Risking guilt by association, loss of position and future, they stepped out to do the right thing for this stranger from Galilee.

But there are two more!

Claudia and Joanna: Matthew 27:11–26

We must look at **Pilate's wife, Claudia,** first, for she is named in the key passage. What really motivated her to get involved in this trial? It may have been the precarious status of her husband's career. Pilate was unpopular with the Jewish leaders and viewed suspiciously by his Roman superiors—clear up to Caesar Tiberius himself.

Assignment to govern the difficult and distant land of Israel was not a thing to be desired by a Roman politician. Judea was considered a troublesome place under direct Roman rule, and ripe for uprisings. Pilate had a background of questionable heritage, and had shown murderous behavior. On arriving at his assigned post, Pilate soon angered the Jewish religious leaders and constituency by erecting imperial images and encouraging emperor worship and pagan games. He confiscated temple tax money for government improvements and insulted the Jews in many other ways. The Jewish leaders had already appealed to Caesar for his dismissal, and he was being watched by all sides. Given these circumstances, Claudia may merely have been trying to save her own, and her husband's, future by intervening.

A wife has the doubtful privilege of discerning her husband's character more intimately than others can. In her years of marriage, Claudia may have become painfully aware of Pilate's bent to cowardice. This man knew, by his own testimony, that Jesus was innocent (see Matthew 27:3–4 and Luke 13–16). Yet knowing the facts, he still caved in to the Jews. When the Barabbas tradeoff failed, he washed his hands in symbolic innocence and let them have what they wanted. Claudia may have hoped to turn his head before the sentence was final.

Perhaps, as she claimed, she actually had a dream. She had likely known that, during the evening before, the Jews came to her husband for a guard to accompany the temple troops in the arrest. If she were a Jewish sympathizer, and perhaps inquiring into following Christ, the action would have disturbed her and could have prompted a dream. We know from Scripture that God used—and maybe still uses—dreams to communicate in certain situations. Those events alone could have motivated her to dream—and then convey her warning to her husband during the early morning trial.

But we also know intuitively that there was a whole subculture of women involved in Jesus' life and the events of that weekend. Their story is not well told in the Scriptures, because it was not central to the events we need to know. There were women in the throngs of Jesus' followers at the triumphal entry parade, women in the temple court when he cleansed it, and women who listened to the confrontations of Jesus and temple leaders. There were women with the Disciples, women married to the Jewish Sanhedrin and political leaders, women everywhere present and involved. These women also had a part in the events of the Cross, and it is there we go to ask, "What would I have done in Joanna's place?"

Joanna, too, risked her husband's career to even be identified as a believer. She is one of our few clues that there were followers of Christ in the higher ranks of Judaism. She, along with Joseph of Arimathaea, and Nicodemus. We must wonder, could Cuza also have been a secret disciple? If not, why would he have allowed his wife to go traipsing about Galilee after an itinerant evangelist? (See Luke 8:1–3.) Giving his money to the cause? Disclosing her faith by being at the Cross and the burial? (Study Luke 23:55–56 and 24:9–11.) Whether or not she ever had any conversations with Claudia, as our story has conjectured, Joanna was a courageous woman who took her stand at the Cross with the Savior she loved and believed to be the Messiah.

Touch Point

Courage in these stories is certainly the *operative word*, as they say. In the midst of this awful miscarriage of justice some women stood up and spoke out by their words and actions. Risking career, marriage, reputation, and future favors, Joanna and Claudia were among the brave ones. We must ask the unanswerable question: *Given those circumstances, would I have been counted with those who spoke out for the Lord?* More importantly: *Am I so counted in my world today?*

As hostility to our faith grows and taking a stand for *any* moral absolute is often considered intolerance or bigotry, we risk even more to live and speak out our values as Christians. It isn't cool, it isn't popular, it isn't wanted, and it may not be heard or accepted. Yet, holding to the teachings and values of Scripture against what we see around us in the media, in the culture of our children and grandchildren, in our neighbors and coworkers, we often find ourselves of the minority opinion. To speak out is to be labeled "out of it," "old," and "old-fashioned." But, look around as you stand alone for the unpopular view. There beside you stands Joanna, a woman for every age. And know this: Everyone will not hear you, but the ones to whom God has sent you will hear.

Chapter 15

Extravagant Love

Mary of Bethany
(John 12:1–19 and 11:17–27)

The minute he came through the door Mary knew something was terribly amiss. Tragedy veiled his face and glazed the life from his eyes.

"Brother, what has happened? You look awful," she whispered, taking his travel bag as he swung it off his shoulder. Lazarus sank onto the couch in silence, pulling off his turban and laying it on the cushion at his side. Shaking his head sadly, he stared down at the floor.

"Brother?" she tried again, snatching answers out of thin air in an effort to help him. "Talk to me. Did something awful happen in Jerusalem? Were you robbed on the way home?" Now his face was buried in both hands and his shoulders began to shake. Mary knelt by her brother, her hand on his arm. "What has happened?" she asked again softly.

Lazarus looked at his middle sister, and Mary thought she had never seen his eyes look so deep and angry. "They crucified him," he said simply. "He's gone, Mary."

"Who, Brother?"

"He's gone," Lazarus repeated angrily. "Jesus is gone from us. How could they have done such a cruel and senseless thing to such a good man? It makes no sense."

Stunned, Mary fell back on her heels beside him. "What are you saying, Lazarus? They crucified our Jesus? Surely you are mistaken!"

"No, Sis, I'm not. I wish I were. But I saw it myself. The Jews lied to Pilate, and he did it—this afternoon. He knew it was wrong, but he did it. And it was terrible."

Lazarus' head fell into his hands again, and Mary reached to enfold her brother in her arms. For a few minutes they could only hold each other and cry.

Then the questions began to come. "Where are all his men?" she asked.

"They fled in fear. Only John stayed."

"And his mother?"

"With John somewhere. Jesus gave her to him from the Cross."

"Did Mary have to see it?" The thought brought her pain.

"I think she stayed to see it. She couldn't leave him. John tried to take her away, but…"

"Dear God!" she murmured. "Poor, dear Mary. And Peter?"

"I don't know. John said Peter tried to stay, but they were onto him, and he is hiding out. I'm sure he will be back—in time."

Sadness and despair began to creep through Mary as she rubbed the knot in her stomach. Finally she could not deny the awful reality of the news. Laying her head on her arms, she sobbed against the soft cushions of the couch. Lazarus patted her shoulder, letting her have her tears. "I'm sorry, Sis. I'm sorry. There was nothing we could do. Soldiers everywhere…." His voice trailed into silent despair.

"I guess Joseph and Nicodemus will bury him this evening," he sighed. "When I left for home they had gone to Pilate for permission. Sabbath was beginning, and I didn't stay. Jesus was already dead two hours." Lazarus lay back on the couch and covered his eyes with his sleeve, as if to blot from his mind the terrible hours just past.

"You must be totally spent," Mary comforted. "Just rest a while. Martha has gone next door to take dinner to Dorcas. You will need to tell her the sad, awful news when she comes back. Then we will think about some supper." She walked to the shelf to get a blanket to cover her only brother.

"I'm just so sorry you had to see him killed," she said gently. "But I am proud of you for staying. You were in danger, too, you know. Every Jew in the Council knows Jesus raised you from the dead—and hates you for it." But her words went unheard. By the time she walked back to cover him, Lazarus had fallen into an exhausted sleep.

Mary blew out one of the lamps, then sat numb in the evening light watching her brother. In her deepest heart she had known it was coming. Had Jesus not told her when he was there for dinner just five days earlier? Had he not said he would be put to death at the feast? She had so hoped he was wrong. That the Jewish leaders would be prevented from hurting him. That the great crowds who paraded him into Jerusalem that next day would protect him from the insanely jealous schemes of the Council. She had so hoped for his Kingdom of kindness and love to become a reality. But all that was gone now.

For some reason, she thought of the vase. Quietly she rose and tiptoed to the room she and Martha shared. In the chest beneath the lamp stand she found and retrieved it carefully, shutting the chest with barely a sound. The cold alabaster brought back warm memories.

Mary was so glad she had followed her heart and emptied the whole pint of nard on Jesus' feet as a gift of love. Removing the cork now, she breathed deeply of the lingering fragrance. Jesus had been so pleased with her extravagance. He had understood her clumsy attempt to thank him for giving her back her brother. As always, he received her love with grace.

Turning over the vase she waited, hoping for one last drop of the sweet red oil to trickle down onto her palm. But none was left. She had spent it all on Jesus five days earlier. "Precious Lord," she whispered to the darkness, "how could you be gone from us so soon? We've only known you a few short months." And, pressing the alabaster to her cheek, she cried again. Deep within herself she solemnly resolved to find and visit his tomb when Sabbath was ended.

Martha came home a few minutes later to a dark and silent house, a sleeping brother, and a tearful sister. "What on earth has happened here?" she asked, alarmed. "Is Lazarus sick again?"

Rousing at her voice, Lazarus sat up, collecting his thoughts enough to respond. Mary stood across the room, waiting for her brother to answer. "No, Sister, I'm fine," he assured her. "But I have terrible, terrible news. They killed Jesus today. Pilate crucified him."

Lazarus and Mary searched their older sister's face as she soaked in the awful words. Setting down her basket and jar, Martha slumped onto the couch beside her brother. "Are you certain?" she asked at last.

"I saw it. I watched him die." Lazarus' words left no room for doubt. Martha bowed her head, resting it in her hands, shaking it numbly against the shameful, unchangeable truth.

"I knew they would finally do it," she managed, her voice breaking angrily. "They have been after him like a pack of wild dogs since he raised Brother from the dead last winter."

"It should have been me," Lazarus lamented. *"I* should be dead and Jesus alive."

"No! *No,* Brother!" Both sisters were talking on top of each other. "We can't redo the past," Martha said wisely. "God is in control, and he has allowed it this way—for reasons we cannot know or understand. We must trust his wisdom in this."

"But it is strange, Mary added, "that one who is himself the Resurrection and the Life could be snuffed out so quickly by evil men."

A stunned pause brought both Martha and Lazarus to stare at their sister in wonder.

"That's it!" Martha almost shouted. "He isn't really dead at all!"

"He can't die!" Lazarus agreed. "Jesus can't die, because he is the *True Life!* You hit the truth dead center, Mary."

The three were on their feet by now, meeting in the middle of the room, talking all at once. Tears of hope began to flow as Mary's amazing thought mixed with their grief.

"How did he say it when Brother died?" Martha asked her sister. "'Whoever lives and believes in me will never die.' We surely will see him again!"

"He will rise again, just as Lazarus did," Mary said firmly. "After Sabbath, I will visit his tomb. Something glorious is going to happen there."

Behind the Scene
A Study of John 12:1–19 and 11:17–27

Soul Mates from the Start

While only John tells the story of the raising of Lazarus, Matthew and Mark also include this beautiful account of Mary of Bethany pouring out her love and gratitude upon Jesus' feet in fragrant extravagance. (Compare Matthew 26:6–13 and Mark 14:3–9. Note that Luke 7:37–39 recounts a different anointing by another woman in Galilee two years earlier.)

Mary and Jesus had been soul mates from the start. On his very first visit (find it in Luke 10:38–42) she had been unexplainably drawn to him. His gentle spirit and deep insights must have touched something few had ever discovered deep within her soul. While Martha bustled, Mary sat close, every pore of her being open to his Presence, every sense filled with his nearness.

At the untimely death of her brother, Jesus came too late. Martha met him on the road, but Mary, unable to cope and overcome by grief, stayed behind, mourning at the house. When Jesus called for her she came, and their poignant meeting on the road brought them both to fresh tears. Her grief broke his heart, and he groaned with the empathy of a bosom friend (see John 11:32–35). Lazarus had truly been his brother, too. Then the happy ending: Lazarus stumbled out of the grave with his burial wraps still on! At Jesus' suggestion everyone rushed forward to take the scarf from his face and the binding from his hands and feet. And Mary and Martha had their beloved brother back for a time.

How do you thank a friend who gives you back your brother from the grave?

Touch Point

Mary may have had an unusually deep need for Jesus in her life. We have no indication that she was married at this time, and it was not usual or acceptable for a woman to remain single in Jewish society. Could she have been a widow with a grieving heart? A divorcee, shamed in her community? Perhaps handicapped or ill in a way that would discourage her from being married? Was she older, past the *marrying years?* We cannot even guess her situation, but Mary's circumstances may have hollowed out in her soul a deep emptiness that Jesus was uniquely able to fill. Many of us come to Jesus out of deep need.

Have you ever thought of yourself as a "soul mate" of Jesus? What would it take to become that? Do you find it a thing of joy just to be near him? To worship at his feet? Do you seize every opportunity to be in his Presence? To feel his heartbeat? Is being close to Jesus more than a desire—almost an *obsession?*

Mary's Extravagant Gift: John 12:1–8

Two months after Lazarus' death Mary saw her opportunity to say thank you. Stop and read the story in the

Scripture above. Jesus and the Disciples were back in the neighborhood, headed for the fateful Passover in the city nearby. But the joyful community of Bethany insisted on feting him in celebration of the greatest miracle of all—the raising of their friend and neighbor, Lazarus. Simon (known as "Simon the Leper"—had Jesus also healed him at an earlier date?) hosted the event. Martha helped cook and serve; her gift to Jesus was always loving hospitality. Lazarus was an honored guest. And Mary? Likely she was supposed to be with the women helping cook and serve, but at some point in the evening she slipped away and returned with her treasure.

Where had she gotten that pint of nard? Such a treasure was not common, and may indicate to us that this Bethany family were people of some means. At an earlier time the family had come into possession of this incredibly expensive perfumed *oil of spikenard* from India. Think what Mary *could* have done with it. It might have graced her body for the rest of her life—a pint is a lot of perfume! It could have been sold to provide for her and Martha in their old age. Or been saved for their burials. (Come to think of it, why had she not used it on her brother when he died a few months before?) Or, as Judas had complained, it could have been sold to help the poor. But in Mary's desire to honor Jesus all of *those* possibilities were lost.

Approaching his table, her preference was probably to pour the red oil on his head, but at banquets the men reclined closely together, two or three on a couch, heads toward the table and feet extended outward. Reaching his head would have been too disruptive. Deciding instead to anoint his feet, she quietly broke the seal and began to pour out the perfume. When did Jesus sense her presence and become aware that someone was kneeling to pay him honor? How did he respond? Did he turn to watch her over his shoulder? Did their eyes meet? Did he smile? Surely between them this was a moment of deep emotion expressed and understood.

The fragrance was permeating the courtyard's evening air. And then she realized—she had brought no cloth with which to wipe up the excess! Impulsively she pulled the veil from her head and began to use it, allowing her hair to fall unbound and tangle with the cloth as she worked. By now, everyone close by them and others—even those across the terrace—had roused to the occasion. All eyes were on her. As for decorum, all was lost. The gift was overmuch. Her hair was improperly loosed, her presence a distraction. Everyone else was embarrassed for her, but Mary could do no less. And Jesus accepted her excesses with grace, love, and understanding. While Martha and Lazarus eyed one another in hopeless frustration, and Judas acted out his objection to the expense, Jesus insisted, "Leave her alone. She is doing this early for my burial. I won't be with you much longer." Among his close friends, Mary alone had seized the moment and bared before the world her complete devotion to her Lord.

The Gift

Strange Guest, and kind
I cannot take my eyes from Thee,
nor leave the room this day.
O let me stay near Thee, I pray.

Close Friend in grief,
I cling to Thee in faith, and let
my tears fall free. Then hear
a sob—and feel Your falling tear.

Dear Son of God,
how can I say the things within
my heart? The sweet perfume
of love for Thee shall fill the room.

—Janet Burton

The Beginning of the End: John 12:9–19

Jesus was already a wanted man. Now Lazarus' name was also on the Council's list. The evidence was indisputable—a *dead man walking around alive again*. People were flocking to this rabbi who could produce the kind of religion that lived and breathed and had substance. Some had seen the miracle happen with their own eyes; others had only heard about it. Something simply had to be done. Orders were issued for the apprehending of Jesus and Lazarus.

In the face of all this Jesus walked openly with the people, Lazarus at his side, toward the Passover celebration in Jerusalem. The crowds found him, and with joyous indulgence formed a parade to sweep him into the city with praise, honor, popularity, and acclaim. It was Jesus' moment of glory and power, more precious because it did not live long. As his following swelled the opposition grew. It would all be over soon.

The Resurrection and the Life: John 11:17–27

Did Lazarus witness the Crucifixion of his beloved friend and mentor as our story surmised? The Bible account gives us no such indication. By this time he was intimately associated with Jesus and his band. Bethany was less than two miles from Jerusalem, and there is good evidence that Jesus spent several nights of Passover week at the home of Martha in Bethany. (Compare Mark 11:11–14 and 20–21.) It is certainly possible that Lazarus was part of the terrible events that so cruelly took Jesus' life. If not, he would have heard about it from friends soon after.

When the news came on that spring day, the three Bethany friends could not have helped playing back their own experience of death and Resurrection just a few months before. The conversations between Jesus and the sisters en route to Lazarus' tomb had not been forgotten. They had stood within inches of him as a power went forth that raised their brother from death back to life. Better than most of his friends, they understood what "I am the resurrection and the life" meant. Jesus was no ordinary man put to death; he was the very Son of God, the giver of life and the renewer of life. Death did not stop him before, and surely it could not stop him now. The realization must have been electric when it dawned on their minds. Somehow I have to think they knew the Resurrection was coming.

The key, then, and now, is *belief.* "He who *believes* in me will live, even though he dies; and whoever lives and *believes* in me will never die. Do you *believe* this?" (John 11:25–26, italics added). What an incredible promise! Loved ones who die believing in Jesus still live—even if beyond our sight. We who believe in Jesus, even though we die, will continue to live in the "real world," not really dead at all. That's why, for those who believe, Hope walks in and commands the day when a loved one passes from our touch into the arms of the Lord. We can know this. We can *know.*

Touch Point

Have you given Jesus, on occasion, a lavish gift? Expensive beyond reason? Unsolicited and unexplained to others? Not to be seen, not to win a favor, but only to express love and gratitude for his gift of Life to you? Offerings are usual, and tithes are commanded. But gifts—whether of time, possessions, or abilities—are from the heart, and are very personal expressions of the soul. We are better people for having squandered something so precious on our beloved Lord just because we

cannot stop ourselves—and with no motive but love. That's what soul mates do!

Chapter 16

Mourning Breaks

Mary Magdalene
(John 19:25–20:18)

The two walked in silence through the late evening twilight, huddled together like frightened children. Where possible they moved in deep shadows, avoiding lighted doorways and courtyards ablaze with holiday fires. Sabbath had begun, and the devout ones were gathering in their homes for prayer.

"The house is close now," Mary Magdalene encouraged her friend. "We are almost there." She nudged the other Mary into an alley just behind the fish shop. "This is a shortcut. John showed it to us yesterday."

"Good!" Mary Clopas whispered. "I'm so tired I jump at every noise." The two hurried on, eager to be inside and out of the sight of soldiers or guards who might eye them with suspicion. After the events of the last two days, who could hope to be safe?

Reaching their borrowed home, the women climbed the outside stairway to an upstairs room and tapped gently on the door. Shortly they heard the bolt slide back, and the door opened just a crack. "Peter?" the Magdalene said. "It's Mary and me."

"No, it's Simon," came the reply, and the door opened wider. "Come in quickly. We were afraid for you!"

The two stepped over the threshold and into the arms of their distressed friends. "Thank God you are both safe," sobbed Salome. "We have been so worried for you!" Someone secured the bolt behind them.

"Were you hiding?" Andrew asked, concerned. "We thought you might have run into danger."

Mary Magdalene loosed her veil from her face, letting it fall to her shoulders as she answered. "No. We stayed to see him buried...and it took a while." Everyone fell silent. "Where is Peter?" she asked, searching the group quickly.

"Hiding out, we think," Thomas answered. "They let Joseph have the body, then?" His surprise was evident.

Mary Clopas nodded. "Yes. We were all amazed. But Joseph and Nicodemus have connections. Pilate released Jesus to them just before Sabbath...not long after John and Mary left."

"Oh, Nicodemus helped with the burial?" Thomas pursued. "That surprises me even more!"

"Us, too," Mary Magdalene agreed. "But it was a good thing. It took both of them, along with two of Joseph's servants, to carry the body to the tomb."

A low wail came from the far corner, where Jesus' mother lay resting on a mat. "Did they bury him well?" she sobbed. "My poor, poor son. Oh, my Jesus! Why did they hurt you? Why did they take you from me?"

Mary Magdalene went to kneel beside her friend. "Yes, dear," she comforted, embracing Mary and holding her close like a child. "Joseph had a new tomb that had never been used, and new linens he gave, and many pounds of spices…"

"Probably over a hundred pounds of spices…" The other Mary also came to kneel by the anguished mother.

"Joseph and Nicodemus wrapped him well," Mary Magdalene assured her. "But Mary Clopas and I will go back when Sabbath is over to be certain all is completed." As she spoke, she rocked the older woman gently back and forth, noticing that her dress had been torn and reversed, in the manner of a grieving mother.

"It was really getting too dark to see well by the time they finished," Mary Clopas concluded.

"My poor Jesus," his mother sobbed again from a heart of inconsolable loss.

John stepped to her side to help, kneeling next to Mary Magdalene, and pressing the suffering mother to his own chest. "I'm here, Aunt Mary," he assured her. "And I'll take care of you now, like Jesus said." Laying her back to the mat, he sat beside her, taking her hand in his. "Sleep now, Aunt Mary." And her sobs began to slowly subside.

The others retreated to the opposite side of the room, sprawling on the floor in various postures. Couches and chairs were still turned to the wall, even though the burial was over.

"It was such a horrendous death." Sadness overtook Mary Magdalene as the terrible memories of the day rushed back. "I could barely stay to see him suffer so. It was a relief when he finally died."

"It could have been worse," Simon answered her. "Sometimes they live two or three days. Only the Romans could think of such a horrible way to kill someone. Barbarians!!" he charged, pounding his fist on the floor. "They are nothing but barbarians!!"

"It's Passover." James was trying to change the subject. "And I'm so glad we ate the meal with Jesus. We sure could not eat it now."

"And Jesus was the Passover lamb." Andrew's soft voice caused them to think. "Killed by the priests for their own sins!"

"Which are many!" Simon could not contain his rage.

"Killed for us all, really," Andrew gently corrected himself. "The Lamb of God who takes away the sins of the world—our sins, too."

"The scapegoat lamb, I guess," the other Mary ventured.

"No, the True Sacrifice," Andrew finished. Again they sat in silence for several minutes, trying to make sense of a day gone wrong. A life snuffed out without just cause. A dream crushed.

"It's late," James said, standing, "and it's getting cool. Let me help you four ladies downstairs to your beds. We eleven will sleep up here again tonight, taking turns at the watch."

"Just ten," Matthew corrected. "Peter is still out, and, of course, Judas…"

"Curse Judas!" Simon spat on the floor. James laid a heavy hand on his shoulder.

John roused Jesus' mother and brought her to the stairs. "Care for Aunt Mary tonight," he admonished his mother as he started down. "Call if you need me in the night."

Salome nodded her intention to watch over her sister and turned to scan the group. "Does everyone have a cloak or shawl or something for cover?" she asked.

Salome and John helped Mary down the inside steps to her bed. Everyone moved slowly and numbly to his or her mat. Then the house grew very still, except for a lamp flickering here and there. Damp cold crept in around the closed doors and shutters. The dark seemed thick and comforting, but sleep came hard.

Peter came in sometime during the night. Mary Magdalene found him sitting by the brazier with his brother when she came upstairs the next morning. "Shalom, Peter," she said softly as she saw him. Peter managed a nod, but could not meet her eyes. "I'm glad you are back," she said, quietly touching his back as she passed. Andrew hung a calloused hand around his brother's shoulder.

The Sabbath dragged by slowly and quietly. No one mentioned food. Salome put dishes of flatbread, cheese, and olives on the table, but it mostly went untouched. James suggested they not go to the temple that day, much to everyone's relief. Quiet conversations alternated with graphic memories and times of angry tears. At some point the couches and chairs were turned around for the older ones to use. And always they listened for the step that would not come, and the Voice that did not speak.

Late in the day Peter dispatched three of the younger men to the tomb to check on any activity by the authorities. On their return Little James reported that Roman soldiers were standing guard, and Pilate's seal had been made on the stone. "Are the soldiers there to keep us out, or to keep Jesus in?" asked Peter cynically. No one ventured an answer.

"If the stone is sealed," Mary Magdalene worried aloud, "then how will Mary Clopas and I check on his body in the morning? We had planned to buy spices and go back after Sabbath, but we dare not break the seal."

"What good would that do?" Peter challenged. "Dead bodies don't go anywhere. And the stone is way too heavy for you to move, anyway."

"And, you said Joseph and Nicodemus buried him well," Matthew agreed. "Why buy more spices and put yourselves at risk by going where the soldiers are?"

The women exchanged glances and Mary Magdalene answered. "His mother will want to visit the tomb once or twice before we all start back for Galilee. We just wanted to be sure it was done well before she saw him."

"Where will you get spices?" James persisted. "All the shops are closed for Sabbath. And Judas is gone…along with our purse." Absently he stroked his beard and shook his head at the thought.

"This evening after Sabbath's end some shop will be open. And I still have some money. I knew not to give it all to Judas. Before morning comes, we'll be ready," Mary assured him.

Salome watched and listened from several feet away. "I'd like to go with you, Mary," she said to her friend. "I'd like to see where he has been laid."

"Well, whatever," Peter said with a shrug of resignation. "But count me out. When this feast is over, I'm heading home to Capernaum. There are still fish in the sea, and someone has to make a living for this group."

Behind the Scene
A Study of John 19:25–20:18

Sorting Out the Marys

Mary must have been the trendy name in the closing years of the B.C. era. Both our story—and the New Testament itself—are full of women called Mary. The best known of these were:

Mary of Nazareth: The virgin mother of our Lord Jesus who entertained angels, married a carpenter named Joseph, and later had other sons and daughters (see Matthew 13:55–56). We will meet her again in the next chapter.

Mary of Bethany: Whom we met in the previous chapter, sister of Martha and Lazarus, who anointed Jesus with expensive perfume (John 12:1–3).

Mary Magdalene: Or, Mary from Magdala. She is usually listed first in the "women from Galilee" who traveled with Jesus and his band, ministering to their needs. (See Luke 8:1–3.) She was one of the first to see Jesus after the Resurrection. More about her later in this chapter.

Mary, Mother of James and Joses: Also known as "the other Mary," or "the wife of Clopas." (Compare Matthew 27:55–56, 28:1, Mark 15:47 and 16:1, and John 19:25.) She was at the Cross, at Jesus' burial and Resurrection, as we saw in the above vignette.

Mary, Mother of John Mark: A member of the fledgling Jerusalem church, in whose home the congregation often met. Hers may also have been the home where Jesus and the Disciples observed the Last Supper and awaited the Spirit at Pentecost (see Acts 12:12).

Forgiven Much, She Loved Much: Luke 8:1–3

Let's focus here on the Mary of this chapter, Mary Magdalene. Luke tells us she was one of those who had been cured by Jesus of evil spirits and diseases. More specifically, "from whom seven demons had come out." Do you wonder what those demons may have been? What they had been doing inside her mind and body? What she had suffered before she came to believe in and follow the Lord?

The whole subject of demons within and without is difficult for us to sort out in this more enlightened time. After centuries of discoveries by scientists and medical researchers, we know much that the Bible people did not know about diseases, germs, mental problems, and physical cures. These discoveries have been allowed us by God. They are his gifts to us, and they have opened up for us better ways to cope and find healing. We generally do not speak seriously in terms of demons today, and many choose to believe that they were simply a product of the ignorance of that earlier age. (The belief is common in primitive cultures and religions of our age.) What seems certain is that evil and invisible forces can come against our minds and bodies and cause disruption and dysfunction in our lives—even today. We also know that the power of Jesus is stronger than demons and can conquer them whenever the two forces collide in a showdown.

We speak more lightly of "demons" now. When we have a down day, when old memories rob us of joy, when bad habits and unchecked emotions take charge, we wink impishly, reach for an aspirin, and say we are "fighting our demons." I see danger in treating the subject of demons so glibly. It may cause us not to take seriously the very real battle we must continually fight in our souls against evil. It might disguise for us our constant responsibility to call on the power of God's Spirit within, to "put on the whole armor of God" and "resist the devil." We must be on guard never to wink at the power of Satan, for he is alive and well in our world.

That said, we may well ask, "What demons commonly come against the women in polite society today? What invisible, destructive spirits can shatter our mental health? Destroy the peace of our homes? Disrupt our families? Control our mental processes so that we cannot function in a whole and productive way?" Our "demons" may not be the same as those Jesus cast out of Mary Magdalene, but they are very real to us on the days they arrive to take charge. Here are a few.

All of us know well the "demon" of **Fear**—the spirit that paralyzes us with the *what ifs* and *I can'ts* of life. God gave us fear to caution us against foolishness and to trigger our good sense and good judgment. But sometimes, perhaps through early failures and tragedies, the over-schooling of conscience, or other factors, women can become bound, obsessed, and unable to function in the normal risks and relationships of life. Fear is literally in control, limiting all they say and do.

Another healthy spirit gone awry is **Guilt.** God intended it to bring us to confession and needed changes in behavior and thought. Using guilt in this way, we gain forgiveness and move on to be wiser and stronger women. But it can become an immobilizing inner controller that is used effectively by Satan and his forces to make us feel totally unworthy of love from God and others.

Abuse can be a kind of "demon" that keeps us from abundant life. Abuse in early years is forced upon us by unthinking (or evil) adults and older siblings who "use us" for their ends. It comes by words, by attitudes, by neglect and bullying actions. It is a scarring and damaging reality in the lives of many women. Sadly, abuse suffered from others can later result in self-inflicted, crippling habits that make a person increasingly sicker until help arrives.

Anger and **Rage** are dominating "demons." They may grow in our minds as a result of abuse such as that just described, or through inherited qualities of personality gone unchecked. Circumstances may trigger the latent tendencies. Mental illness—not of our own making—may cause these emotions to go out of control. God gave us anger in order to defend ourselves against dangers, but in its worst scenario it puts us in prison. It feeds on unhealthy rumination and can keep us locked up internally in the turmoil of resentment and suspicion.

Depression is one of the best-known "demons" of all. Depression puts us in a fog of recycling thought patterns, a box of self-imposed seclusion, a bed of paralysis. Depression may be anger turned inward on ourselves, or anger bottled up, unexpressed towards others. It may be a chemical problem, unbalancing the brain and clouding the mind. Depression, in the normal ebb and flow of life, is expected. But in its crippling form, it holds a person hostage to the inner self.

Lust and **Jealousy** are twin spirits of Satan, both desiring strongly what they cannot and should not have. Ambition is the healthier side—creating a dream and a desire to work for what can be. Lust and jealousy eat at a woman from the inside, creating fantasies of worlds that should not be. They turn love and friendship into unwholesome relationships, coloring every thought and act with greed. All about us in our world we find these evil spirits taunting us and others.

A Clearer Picture of Mary

Whether these were some of the "seven demons" Jesus cast out of Mary Magdalene, or whether hers were more serious incapacities, we can only speculate. Because we first meet her in Luke 8:1–3, traditionally she has been linked with the prostitute whose story precedes in Luke 7:36–50. Predictably, Hollywood has fostered that idea. We found it in the musical and the movie *Jesus Christ Superstar*, and other popularizations of the gospel. But historians reject that idea as groundless. For evidence they point out that a woman so mentally ill as to have "seven demons" probably could not have functioned in that profession very well. Others misinterpreted her as the secret wife of Jesus, as in Dan Brown's fiction novel, *The DaVinci Code*, built on spurious information that is still unsubstantiated. Earlier groups, such as the Gnostics of the first Century, cast her as a disciple, more powerful even than Peter. Poor Mary! Too bad she cannot come back to defend herself. Bible truth portrays her only as a deeply devoted friend and follower of Jesus, who traveled with the women disciples and was present at the Cross and at the Resurrection.

What we do learn from Luke 7:47 is this: The one who is forgiven much, loves much. And that is surely true of Mary Magdalene. She loved Jesus so much that she left her former life, cast her lot and fortune with him and his Disciples, and traveled with them around Galilee, seeing to their daily, practical needs. What do you suppose that entailed? Probably buying and cooking their meals, washing and mending garments, bandaging wounds, and offering cures when they were ill. Do you think she may also have counseled women and children who came to hear Jesus teach?

In the process, Mary lived through two years of awesome experiences. She almost certainly saw the five thousand supernaturally fed and was close when Jesus healed Jairus' daughter, stilled a storm, and walked on water. She met and knew Jesus' family. She heard firsthand about The Transfiguration within hours of its happening, and listened to many of the same parables and teachings Jesus gave his men, preparing them for their mission to come. And she surely saw the opposition of the Jewish leaders and the gathering storm soon to break upon them at Passover.

When the women are listed (as in Luke 8:1–3, or in accounts of the Cross, Christ's burial, and his Resurrection), Mary Magdalene is usually named first. Perhaps she was the most prominent, a natural leader, the hardest worker, or the best-loved by the gospel writers. But we can be certain that, from her former life of brokenness, Mary became a valued servant and friend of the Lord.

Touch Point

Mary should give us great hope, for who among us has not felt brokenness to some extent? Past mistakes, difficult circumstances, relationship failures—these are used by Satan to convince us that we are useless to God, now and for the remainder of our lives. What a double victory for evil! First, he traps us in the muck of life, and then uses the memories and scars of the experience to render us useless.

How did Mary come to Jesus and experience healing? Whatever the particular place, the conversation, the action, she came in her brokenness. She fell at his feet in desperation and in hope. He forgave her and raised her up to live a productive, vital life. She became one of the most valued women of the gospel story—and one of the most privileged. How good that she did not say, "Oh, not me, Lord.

I'm not worthy to follow you. Let me just stay home and keep a low profile, lest some shame come upon you for associating with me."

Are we listening here? How dare some tell us, "Women are not called to take their places beside men in serving Jesus." "Women with a 'past' must live in the shadows for fear of disgracing the church." Mary Magdalene's life shouts another message. Listen to the heart of Jesus! He heals, and forgives, and "remembers it no more." He gives life after brokenness! And he calls women to follow him into ministry to others.

The Bleak Desperation of Her Loss: John 19:25–40

How much of Jesus' slanted trials, the undeserved abuse, the cruel Crucifixion, did she see? All the gospels place her "near the Cross," or, "standing at a distance." Was she with the women who followed him to the Cross, mourning and wailing (Luke 23:27–31), those to whom Jesus prophesied the destruction of the city soon to come? Did she see Simon of Cyrene conscripted to carry the Cross when Jesus' bloody back and beaten body could no longer bear the load? Was she close enough to hear the hammers pound, or call encouragement to him as he refused the pain-killing vinegar that was lifted to his mouth? Did she see his clothing stripped from him and awarded in a dice game? (Perhaps she had a part in making that very robe, and surely she had laundered and mended it for him.) Did she watch as the ridiculing sign was pounded above his throbbing head? And hear the jeering priests and leaders spit insults in his face?

Surely she stood beside Mary as Jesus gave his mother over to John's care. Surely she held her friend close and added her own sobs to the grieving mother's as darkness fell over the earth. Her heart must have broken as she heard Jesus cry in agony, "My God, my God, why have you forsaken me?" Her arms must have ached to soothe his swollen tongue, cool his fevered brow, and cover his broken body as it hung exposed to the world. A more terrible day she could not have imagined. The Light of the World, and the light of her life, was snatched away in such a cruel, vindictive, inhumane way. Finally the earth itself rebelled, and an earthquake shook the very foundation upon which friends and foes stood watching the awful scene. Creation responded to its Creator's pain.

Others gradually left that day, but the faithful women disciples, numbed by shock, held captive by love, stayed on. When evening covered him, Joseph of Arimathea stepped quietly forward and asked Pilate for the body to provide a decent burial. Coming with friends to claim Jesus, he found the women still at the Cross, guarding the lifeless form of their Master and friend. Jesus' body was lowered and carried to a garden tomb. The loyal women followed, noting the location, watching the linen wrapped about him, seeing the stone secured, and perhaps helping as they could. Reluctantly they turned in the twilight toward their borrowed home.

Can you imagine how Mary Magdalene must have felt during that Friday night and the Sabbath to follow?

Have you ever lost the person who meant most to you? On whom your life turned? For whom you lived and breathed? What do you do with a grief like that? Some women get very busy and cover their thoughts with meals to fix, clothing to prepare, a house to clean. They dare not stop—or reality crashes in and smothers them. But on the Jewish Sabbath no such activity was allowed. Mary probably sat with her friends, comforted Jesus' mother, and tried to cope with her broken future. Conversation must have centered on questions like: "What shall we do now?" "Do you think we are also in danger?" "Dare we continue to work for his Kingdom, or should we go back home to what is left of our old lives?" Mary had no old life to go back to—only memories of demons banished and waiting to reclaim her if she let go of the Savior who had filled her life with love and purpose.

Touch Point

Mary as yet grasped little of the hope that awaited her as a believer. Her desire was still for the broken body of her beloved Lord. Her plan of action was to return to the grave as soon as the Sabbath ended, to lovingly add to the spices and wrappings done hurriedly by Joseph. The truth that in letting Jesus go she would have him with her always seems not to have entered her mind.

Does Mary's life not illustrate to us how important it is to have a vital faith when we lose someone we need and love? The bleak

desperation of loss is gentled by an underlying assurance that there is more to life than what we see and feel here. Life goes on beyond this present reality. Reunions await us, and justice will be served. Grief still comes, hard and unyielding, but faith tempers it. As Paul tells us, we "do not grieve like the rest of men, who have no hope" (1 Thessalonians 4:13–18). What a comfort this truth is in such times!

Joy Came In the Morning: John 20:1–18

It was in this mood of black despair that the women came to the tomb at dawn on Sunday morning. We know, because they were not seeking a risen Lord, but a dead friend's mangled body. The four gospel writers all tell the story, though each a bit differently. Putting the pieces together into a whole, we find Mary Magdalene, Mary Clopas, Salome, and Joanna named in the group that made that sad trek. "How ever will we move that huge, sealed grave cover?" they kept asking each other, unaware that an earthquake in the early morning hours had dislodged it, revealing that the greatest miracle of the ages had already taken place.

In the shock, fear, joy, and confusion of discovery, the women could not absorb it all. His body had somehow been taken and was missing—yet the grave clothes were undisturbed! Men dressed in brilliant white were guarding the tomb. Soldiers lay stunned on the ground. "He is not here; he has risen from the dead," the angel stated. The words made little sense to them, and all the women could do was turn and run for help.

We can wonder if Mary Magdalene ran first and fastest, because when Jesus met them on the road (see Matthew 28:9–10), it seems that she was not there. But she seems to have been first to get the news to Peter and John (John 20:2). John himself tells of rushing with Peter to Jesus' tomb, to check out Mary's report, and not understanding what had really happened. So they returned home, afraid to believe the best, still fearing the worst.

Mary must have followed them back to the tomb, for when all the others had gone she was compelled to remain alone in the chilly, early morning mist, still looking for the dead body of her Lord. Sleepless nights had clouded her mind, and swollen eyes kept her from seeing clearly the garden about her. Checking the grave again, she saw "men" instead of angels. Turning away in despair, she saw a "gardener" instead of Jesus! Silly woman, we think, but grief does strange things to our minds.

"Mary!"

Her eyes had fooled her, but her ears knew that Voice. It was the Voice that had healed her two years before. The Voice that had taught the deep truths of God, blessed little children, and raised the dead. It was her very own, precious Teacher and Friend!

"Rabboni!"

And she ran forward to embrace him.

"Don't cling to me, for I have to go away," seems to be the message he gives her. "Go tell my brothers that I am alive, and returning to the Father." In a very short moment, it seems, he was gone. Mary now understood, and, forsaking her quest for a dead Savior, she turned to run and tell the Disciples a second time. She had seen and touched the Living Lord!

Why did Jesus choose to visit Mary Magdalene separately in those first hours? Why not Peter, or Thomas, or his mother? Perhaps the depth of her grief betrays the depth of her love, and he knew in his gracious and tender way that she could not be otherwise consoled. Perhaps it confirms that hers was one of the calmer minds of the group. Notice that, not only did he select her to visit with first following his Resurrection, he also chose her to carry an important message to his men. "Go and tell my brothers…" The first time she had gone to them in fear, and they had not believed her. Maybe somewhere in the backs of their minds they harbored the thought, "This once-ill woman is having delusions. Surely she is babbling through her grief." But this second time, how could they deny her joy and certainty? "I have seen the Lord!" said Mary, "and this is what he told me."

Touch Point

Jesus! He comes to us in unexpected places. At the most desperate times of our lives He stands behind us, waiting for us to turn to him, softly calling our names. Making sense out of the broken pieces. Giving direction for the days ahead.

When life falls apart and nothing goes according to your plan, turn around. He is standing nearby. You are not alone!

Chapter 17

Singing Again

Mary of Nazareth, Part 2
(Acts 1:12–2:47)

Mary came downstairs from morning prayers, humming and pulled the shutters open wider. "Where are the others?" she asked a gray cat, perched cozily on the sill. Early summer sunshine flooded the courtyard, where several of her friends had joined the servants in preparing for today's guests and tomorrow's feast. Snatching a handful of grapes from the table, she stepped out the open door and called: "My, you all look busy! How can I help?"

Salome stopped her sweeping long enough to answer her sister. "Well, our hostess seems to have it all under control. Mary Magdalene and Mary Clopas are finishing the grinding. Rhoda did the milking, and the menservants have two lambs on the spit."

"Two lambs?" Mary questioned. "We must be expecting a crowd!"

"We already have a crowd," called Mary Magdalene from her chore of grinding in a shady corner. With the back of her wrist she chased a stray lock of hair from her damp brow. "Just look what we have done to these kind people! There are two dozen of us here already—and more will be arriving for Pentecost today."

"How were morning prayers?" Mary Clopas asked Jesus' mother. "We just couldn't get away with all the company coming."

"Oh…good!" Mary responded. "Peter led us, and everyone was blessed. It is easy to praise God now that we know our Jesus is alive and well and returned to his glory."

As each woman turned back to her work, Mary wandered past the cooking fire and over to a bench in the shade of a pomegranate tree, still humming quietly to herself. Jezebel the nanny clomped across the cobblestones to nuzzle her lap, hoping for a bite of her snack. Mary scratched the goat's head and smoothed her floppy ears gently. "It's all gone, Jezzie. I didn't save you even a bite." Jezzie eyed her coolly.

Little James came down the outer stairs to check the progress of the roasting lambs. "They smell wonderful, James," Mary called. He nodded and met her eyes with a respectful smile.

"Your song is back, Sister," Salome noted. "It's good to hear you sing again."

Smiling, Mary softly began the song she had sung so often these almost thirty-four years: "My soul praises the

Lord and my spirit rejoices in God my Savior, for he has been mindful of the humble estate of his servant. From now on all generations will call me blessed."

Salome picked up the familiar words and joined her sister's song. "For the Mighty One has done great things for me. Holy is his Name!"

"He certainly has done that!" exclaimed the Magdalene, "Great things for you, Mary dear, and for us all, and more wonderful things are sure to come. Does Peter have any more idea when the Comforter will arrive?"

"No," Mary turned toward her younger friend. "Maybe tomorrow, on the feast day. Maybe later. We must just wait and pray. Jesus will keep his word; he always does."

Chores continued through the middle of the day. It was early afternoon before their hostess called the men upstairs to wash for dinner. Salome and the Marys were already there to help with the serving. It was a full table with the Twelve, joined by the men of the household, along with the two younger brothers of Jesus, who had returned with the group from Galilee. Mary could scarcely keep her song quiet as she saw her two boys take their places with the Disciples. Years of conflict had melted and vanished now that James and Joseph had finally believed. *My soul magnifies the Lord,* she sang joyfully in her heart.

"Blessed art thou, Eternal our God, King of the Universe, who has kept us in life, and has preserved us, and enabled us to reach this season," chanted the men in unison. And the meal began. Pentecost was always a happy season for men, with the work of the field behind them and the barns full of barley for the year ahead. An even greater joy surrounded these men and women, who now waited in quiet expectation for The Promise.

Matthias, newest of the Twelve, was reclining across from the Lord's brothers. "So you two did not believe that Jesus was the Messiah?" he asked with casual bluntness.

Mary, reaching to fill an empty breadbasket, froze at his brash words. Finally James broke the tension, never looking up from his plate. "It took us a while," he admitted.

"After that mess up at the synagogue in Nazareth we were so embarrassed we didn't even want to admit he was our brother," Joseph defended. "That wasn't your everyday picture of who a Messiah would be."

"He was a bit feisty that day, as I recall," Andrew offered. "I wouldn't call it a 'mess up,' but we were all a bit taken aback by his statements. I can see how that would have upset the family more than a little." Mary continued her task, listening carefully. Andrew was always so gentle in the awkward times.

"They nearly threw him down Lookout Hill," James reminded them. "It was a bad scene."

"So what turned your minds?" Matthias persisted. "When did you believe?"

Joseph looked at this older brother and nodded. James put down his sop and eyed the newcomer squarely. "When we saw him in Galilee last month, walking on the shore, cooking breakfast, acting like it was the usual thing to be raised from the dead."

"He was just the same," Joseph insisted, "except for the scars. There was no mistaking the scars. There was just no other choice than to believe."

"It all makes sense to us now," James added. "Everything fell into place when I saw him on the beach. So...here we are," and he poked the last of the sop in his mouth.

Salome caught her sister's eye and smiled behind their backs. "And your mother is very glad," she ventured.

Joseph reached back to grab Mary's sleeve and give it a playful tug. "Mothers never quit, do they, Aunt Salome?" he agreed. "She prayed for us and loved us all the way. She gets a lot of credit for that."

"Mother believed in Jesus when we boys could not," James conceded. "She's a very brave lady."

"Stubborn...but brave," Joseph teased, and to Mary's relief the conversation ranged on to other topics.

The meal was almost over when a craggy voice called through the partially-open door at the top of the stairs. "Is this the Jesus House? May a weary old sinner join you for a bite to eat?"

"Zacchaeus!" Thomas declared, without even seeing him. "Zacchaeus, come in this place!" And in walked the best-dressed tax man in the territory.

"Can a weary old sinner get a meal here?" he repeated with pretend contrition.

Matthew got up from his couch to welcome his old friend. "Shalom, Zacchaeus!" he said, and embraced him warmly. "You are here for tomorrow's temple feast, I guess. Yes! Join us for some dinner."

"Thank you," the strange little man responded, noting that all the places at the table were taken. Simon, a former Zealot, quickly gave the guest his place on Matthew's couch. Grabbing one last piece of bread, Simon backed up to the place where several of the younger ones squatted against a wall, secretly happy to put a little distance between himself and the infamous Roman sympathizer.

"You knew about his Resurrection?" Peter quizzed Zacchaeus.

"Both the death and the Resurrection," Zacchaeus quickly assured them. "Word travels fast at the feast time—all the travelers, you know. And Jericho isn't that far from Jerusalem. Heard it over and over again. Must have been awful for you."

"Awful then, but joyful now," John observed, as heads nodded all around.

Mary left to go downstairs as everyone began talking at once about memories still painful for her to hear. Even the joy of seeing Jesus again could not fully erase the agony of his suffering and death. Deep scars had been carved in her soul. And though he was safe, still her mother's heart longed for his Presence beside her. For his voice, his touch. Salome followed her, reading her thoughts. Sitting at the downstairs table, the two sopped bread and lamb stew silently. Words were not needed between these sisters whose families had shared so much in recent months.

Rhoda, the housemaid, came in with a basket of bread and a bowl of stewed figs, and set it quietly between them.

"Who else are we expecting?" Mary asked, finally.

"Well, Martha and her family," Salome began, "and some other families of the Twelve who are spending today with nearby relatives and friends to take the load off this house."

"We can thank them for that!" Mary said quickly, and Rhoda giggled.

"And several other friends from Galilee who are coming to Pentecost said they might come by for prayers this evening or in the morning," Salome continued.

Mary Magdalene came in from checking the cooking fire and joined them. "I guess the men are all satisfied, and now we women can grab a bite," she said. "Were you talking about the guests who still may come? I hope the food holds out until tomorrow's cooking."

"And I hope the guests bring some with them," Salome added. "This could turn out to be a burden to our hostess."

"Oh, don't fret about that, Miss," Rhoda volunteered. "My mistress has plenty and more, and we are happy to share." A bell at the front gate sent the servant girl hurrying away. In just a minute she returned, smiling, with Martha and Mary of Bethany close behind. Warm greetings and blessings were shared around, as Rhoda quickly came and went with extra baskets and platters to feed the newest guests.

Lazarus had gone up the outer stairs to join the men's meal, and Martha and Salome were soon deep in conversation about cooking for the feast day crowd. At the other end of the table Jesus' mother watched quietly while Mary Magdalene and Mary of Bethany spoke of Jesus.

"How are you, Mary dear?" Mary of Bethany turned to ask the mother of her Lord. Their eyes met and spoke, their hearts joined in understanding.

Tears of joy overcame the mother. "As the old prophet warned me at Jesus' presentation in the temple, 'a sword has pierced my side, also,' but all that is behind us now," she responded. "All the days of rejection and opposition, all the worries for his life. All the cruelties men could impose. God has 'scattered those who are proud in their inmost thoughts.' Our Jesus is alive, and has gone back to his glory, from where he came to Joseph and me so many years ago."

"And we miss him terribly," the Magdalene added, "but he will return to us soon. The angels assured us of that." Taking the hand of Mary of Bethany, she squeezed it tightly. "Oh, Mary, I would have liked so much to see him caught up in the clouds! John and Andrew described it to us. John said it was even more beautiful than The Transfiguration."

The mother watched in quiet joy as these two who had loved her Jesus so much shared from their hearts what few had ever known.

"And now we wait for the Promise," Mary Magdalene said. "I hope you will be staying over. We will have prayer again today at the ninth hour, which is almost here, and again this evening, and in the morning before the feast. And we can make room in the women's quarters down here."

"We are praying a lot these days," the mother agreed, "waiting for the Comforter, the promise of power that Jesus told of as he ascended. Peter is leading us. You will be blessed if you stay."

"Martha and I will stay," the younger sister answered for both. "Lazarus brought Balaam because he will have to ride home to care for the animals and then return early in the morning, before the pilgrims totally jam the way. This is the biggest week of the year in Jerusalem, you know. The road from Bethany was hopelessly crowded already today."

"Wonderful things are going to happen, Mary," the Magdalene assured, and her Bethany friend nodded in eager agreement. "Power is coming, and people will believe. It will be again as it was on the day Jesus entered Jerusalem in the great parade. And surely then he will return to us, as he said."

"So shall we join the men upstairs and pray for the Promise?" his mother suggested, standing to go. "Surely it won't be long now."

Behind the Scene
A Study of Acts 1:12–2:47

The Intervening Years

This is our second study focused on Mary of Nazareth, the mother of our Lord Jesus. We met her in Chapter 2, when she was a young, pregnant girl, struggling with how to break that news to her fiancé, Joseph, and to her parents. And briefly again in Chapter 3, when Simeon and Anna met the Lord's parents in the temple at Jesus' presentation when he was six weeks old. The many events that happened between that time and the beginning of his public ministry—most of which directly involved his parents or his mother, have not been included in this book. But we can be certain of this: the Mary in today's chapter is very changed from the Mary we met earlier. Her life, though she probably struggled to keep it normal, took many unusual turns. For that reason we must look at this wonderful, remarkable woman again.

We could begin as far back as the startling visit of the Magi. What a shock to this Northern village girl to find strange, richly adorned men in her yard at Bethlehem one spring day! It is thought for two reasons that they must have come after the presentation of the infant Jesus at the temple. First, Mary and Joseph were still poor folks at the temple, where, according to Luke 2:23–24, they chose to give the offering of the poor, "a pair of doves or two young pigeons." Next, Matthew's account tells us they fled by night to Egypt right after the Magi's visit, leaving them no time to visit the temple afterward. Did you notice how God, in his wonderful resourcefulness, provided the expensive gifts of gold, incense, and myrrh, which probably eased the family over the difficult financial years in Egypt and afterwards? (Check Matthew 2:13–15.)

Their harrowing return to Nazareth following the death of Herod the Great, their life with Joseph as the village carpenter, and the birth of several other sons and daughters are all omitted here, but you can find a hint of it in Mark 6:3. (Some consider these added children to be Joseph's by an earlier marriage, or perhaps only cousins of Jesus. We see no indication of that in the Bible, so we have just treated them as younger siblings in our story.)

All of us recall Jesus' second, fateful, visit to the temple when he was twelve years old, found in Luke 2:41–52. The beauty of the story is that it shows us Jesus already had a dawning realization of who he was. We can be nearly certain the stories of his birth—the angel visits, the shepherds, the Magi, the death of the innocent babies of Bethlehem—these had been told around the family table. From these alone, Jesus would have strong leadings about his destiny. We also believe that he had an unusual link with heaven, and know that he was being guided carefully by two fathers as he grew. The hidden connection to every mother in this temple tale is the common fear of losing her child in a crowd. Can you feel Mary's heart beating, hear her labored breath, and read the terror in her eyes as she and Joseph searched for this son that had been given into their care by the Almighty?

At the end of the story Luke assures us of some important things about the family life of Mary, Joseph, and their children. We see here that while Jesus was unmistakably a child of destiny, still there was discipline in their home, and he lived life as a child under parental guidance. We also see that he participated in the normal roles of life as a son, a brother, a neighbor, a school boy, and a worshiper. Have you wondered what it would have been like to parent such a precocious child? How would a mother keep the balance between this gifted son and her other six (or more) children? What sibling rivalries might surface as the younger ones saw their brother developing into a rabbi with a mission?

By the time Jesus left home at about age thirty (Luke 3:23) the family situation must have been stable. Most scholars believe Joseph had already died, since after the temple event he is never again mentioned. Jesus' oldest brothers were most likely competent carpenters who could support the household with the family business. There were four boys to tend to the chores and sisters to help in the home, and Mary was probably well cared for in her Nazarene community.

Touch Point

Life, for Mary, as it does for most mothers, took many unexpected turns. It seldom goes as we were so naively hoping it would when we said, "I do." The perfect children we had planned to raise have minds of their own. The dream house we wanted develops a leaky roof. And the price tags of life overwhelm us. Sickness invades, tragedies disrupt, and reversals come. Life is never predictable or boring!

As the years whirl by and children mature, our roles change to support each new level of need in those we love. Motherhood evolves from total nurture to firm guidance to "hands off" anxiety. About the time our kids "grow up" and leave home we begin to see how God—even in the tragic turns and unanticipated difficulties—has been working out His perfect plan for us and for those we love, molding us into the persons he designed us to become, perfecting qualities within us that we did not know were there. All this becomes "our story," and each of us has her own story. The beauty of it for those who believe is that ours is God's story, also.

But there is a catch! We watch the taillights as the kids drive off into their own lives and think, *"My parenting years are over; my task is done. Now I can rediscover the person I really am—the one that has been hiding under the Mom Role all these years."* But, try as we might we cannot seem to shake off this thing called *mothering* from our souls. Our children remain central to our lives, almost our reason for existing. They may no longer need us, but—*what a shock*—we still need them! And the old saying, "Once a mother, always a mother," turns out to be truer than we'd ever believed. It wasn't just a task after all. It was a life! Mary found that out, too.

Getting Used to a Preacher Son

All through his ministry Jesus came and went from his mother's home, and often visited in nearby towns. We have clear pictures of several of these incidents. The first was at the wedding in Cana, just a few miles from Nazareth (find this story in John 2). It may have been a family occasion, because Mary seems to be somewhat involved in the serving problems—namely the shortage of wine. Jesus and his early Disciples, two of whom were almost certainly his cousins, were also invited. (We are assuming here the common interpretation that says Salome is the sister of Mary, which would make James and John first cousins to Jesus. This view is based on a comparison of the women standing at the Cross: John 19:25, Mark 15:40, and Matthew 27:56.) In her usual way, Mary turned proudly and confidently to her older son for help in the wedding crisis…and was somewhat rebuffed at his response. (Mothers of grown sons come to recognize the arms-length replies that signal independence.) In the end he did help, and she was satisfied—if perhaps a bit embarrassed.

The second incident, told best by Luke, concerns the time Jesus came home and was invited to be a reader in the synagogue service. Fresh from his baptism, and the victory over Satan in the wilderness, Jesus was "pumped" (as our children might say). He was now ready to begin the mission for which he had come to earth. The hometown folks had heard about his miracles and seemed more interested in seeing a show than in hearing what he had come to say. What began as a happy homecoming (see Luke 4:14–15 and verse 22) quickly turned into an angry lynch party (compare Luke 4:28–30). Folks didn't like hearing that sometimes Gentiles were more receptive to God's miracles than his Chosen People had been. "Gentile" was a hot-button word in that place and time. Whether from zeal or by design, Jesus alienated his own townsfolk, and probably deeply embarrassed his family in that hour.

From that time on Mary had to deal with heartbreaking conflict within her family. Jesus gained success, fame, and followers. But his own brothers were not among the believers. Mark tells us (see Mark 3:20–21 and 31–35) that once his family came to rescue him from himself—to bring him home for a decent rest and some good food—but he refused to come with them. Further, he gestured to his newfound followers and said, "Here are my mother and my brothers!" Not the stuff that cheers a mother's heart! Lesser insults than that have seriously threatened to fell family trees. And the rift continued through the next two or more years, as John confirms for us in the argument recorded in John 7:1–10. "For even his own brothers did not believe in him."

How did Mary cope with the conflict? She, of course, did believe in her son. How could a mother forget the visit of an angel? The miraculous birth? The story of the shepherds? The prophecy of Simeon? The visit of the Magi? And all the other confirmations God had given her along the way! With one hand she quieted the anger of her sons in Nazareth, and with the other she reached out to her itinerant rabbi firstborn, trying in vain to bring the two together, to mend the tear in her home and in her heart. Few things distress a mother like seeing her grown children at odds. So we are given to believe, in that agonizing moment of his Crucifixion, that Jesus had good reason to will his mother to his cousin, John. His brothers probably were not there with her in that hour, and very likely they still did not believe. Thank God that this situation was corrected some time between the Cross and Pentecost, as we shall soon see.

Touch Point

Again we see how inescapably the mother's role is that of family peacemaker. Is there a family you know that can live and grow under one roof without some level of conflict? Sibling rivalries go back as far as Genesis, Chapter 4—the very first family story on record—so how did we think we could escape it, or outsmart it, or live above it?

Emerging young adult children are thrown cruelly into a competitive, unfriendly, demanding world. Pressures are great. We try hard not to impose sibling comparisons on them. We don't have to—they do it themselves. Mary even experienced it in the premodern, simple, stripped-down village life of Nazareth. Kids in that day probably raced up and down the main drag on donkeys, wore their hair too long, and drank too much wine on Prom Night. We can only guess what kind of balancing act Mary maintained to keep peace between her several sons (and possibly daughters-in-law).

We all wish to be Super Moms and raise our children so wisely and so lovingly that none of the unpleasant emotions have room to grow in their hearts. Although Mary raised a perfect child, she was not perfect herself. She undoubtedly made mistakes, misjudgments, even grievous omissions. Jesus turned out well for many reasons, but Mary's other

sons turned out well also. "My strength is made perfect in weakness," God reminded Paul (2 Corinthians 12:9), and that is a good verse for mothers, too. We are never able to do what we're called to do, but God makes us able to do so by his power working through our lives.

Preparing for Pentecost: Acts 1:12–26

It is now almost Pentecost, fifty days after Jesus' sacrificial death and astounding Resurrection on Passover weekend. (Pentecost is related to the word for fifty, and was also called "the week of weeks," signifying that seven weeks—or fifty days—had passed since Passover.) Mary had seen Jesus resurrected and had almost certainly been with John in the vicinity of the Upper Room appearances (John 20:19 and verse 24). In the intervening weeks the Disciples, following Jesus' instructions, returned to Galilee and there experienced the miraculous catch of fishes, as well as an intimate breakfast with him on the shore (see Matthew 28:16–20 and John 21:1–14). Surely Mary knew of all this…and may have seen some of it firsthand.

Now, following Jesus' directions again, the band returned to the Jerusalem area for his anticipated return to his Father. (Luke gives us details on this in Luke 24:50–53, and in his second letter, Acts 1:1–11.) How old was Mary when all this transpired in her life? We tend to believe she was in her late or mid teens when Jesus was born. Add his thirty-three years to that, and we have a lady only about fifty years old. Motivated strongly to be with her son in these closing days of his earthly life, she could have made those trips quite well in a group of supportive friends.

Finally Jesus' plan was beginning to penetrate the thinking of the group. In some way he "opened their minds" so that they could understand better than they had before. In the urgency of the hour they listened intently and understood that they were to continue the work of establishing his Kingdom through personally witnessing about what they had seen and experienced. The task would be immense—encompassing not just Jerusalem and Judea, but neighboring states and countries and continents. They would be going not just to the Jews, but to "all the world," as far as civilization would allow them to go. And travel in that day extended north to England and east, around Africa, to India! To enable them to travel this extensively, special power would be given them through the coming of the Holy Spirit—the Spirit of Jesus himself. Jesus had been saying these things all along, but somehow the Disciples just did not get it until now.

After making all this clear, Jesus was gloriously "taken up" and enveloped in the clouds, not to be seen again in his physical form during the lifetime of any member of the group. That bittersweet moment was made more bearable by the promise, "This same Jesus, who has been taken from you into heaven, will come back in the same way you have seen him go into heaven."

Full of joy, anticipation, and trepidation, the band returned to Jerusalem, to the Upper Room, and began to prepare themselves in prayer for the awesome, unknown events soon to come. Acts 1:14 is a very exciting verse for our study of Mary. The women were fully included in the times of prayer and Mary, the mother of Jesus, was individually named as being present! But that's not all! Look! His brothers were also listed with the believers! As Paul later records his knowledge of the story, Jesus had made a special appearance to his brother James at some time during those days (see 1 Corinthians 15:7). Could that have been the turning point that brought them into the believers' camp? We can only guess.

For a week the group prayed. Luke also indicates that they spent part of each day at the temple (Luke 24:52–53). And, by the time the Day of Pentecost actually arrived, there were about a hundred and twenty believers together in that place! (Reread Acts 1:15 if you missed that amazing number). Now, who do you suppose was in that group? Begin with the family of Jesus, then add the family in the host home (likely John Mark's home, reviewing Acts 12:12). Next add the Twelve, along with some of their wives and mothers, and also the women from Galilee, and we are close to thirty. Others had come from Galilee for the feast. Some had been there at the Cross. Then there could have been those Jesus had healed, like the man at the Pool of Siloam, and the man born blind. Add those from Jericho, just a few miles away: Zacchaeus and Bartimaeus. And those from Bethany—the family of Martha, and all the neighbors who celebrated the raising of Lazarus. Could Nicodemus and Joseph of Arimathea have been present? What about some of the soldiers from the Cross and the tomb? And were there any from the crowd that had shouted "Hosanna" at Christ's triumphal entry of Jerusalem seven weeks before? Many of these are educated guesses, but some are almost certainly correct. Jesus' fledgling church was about to take wings and fly!

The Day Finally Arrived: Acts 2:1–14

Now read Acts 2:1–14 with new eyes. What a joyful, incredible day! And there is our Mary, right in the middle of it all! For they were "all together" on that day, and, "all of them were filled with the Holy Spirit." All of them, "both men and women" experienced the outpouring of God's Spirit (see verses 17 and 18). And all of them saw the miracle of three thousand people coming to believe in Jesus as Savior and Messiah on one day! Is this not the most wonderful way to end our story of Mary, the mother of Jesus?

Filled and Overflowing

Mary was just a little late joining the group for morning prayers. With all the excitement and preparations of the day before, she had slept until the sun was almost up over Olivet. Listening quietly, she could hear guests arriving as she dressed and hurried up the inside steps. Still wrapping her veil as she came in, she found a space beside Simon, near the very back of the large room. Peter and Matthew were conferring in low tones at the front, probably, she surmised, about plans for sacrificing at the temple later that day.

Looking over the group gathered for prayer, Mary was delighted to see that so many believers had joined them for this feast day. An excitement filled the room as friends touched and hugged and shared happy greetings with each other. Peter stood up to begin leading and a quiet anticipation fell over the room.

"Brothers and sisters, you know we…." But at that moment, from somewhere outside the house, a strange noise began to overpower them. At first she thought it was several chariots rushing over the cobblestones below, but as it grew in intensity Mary could not remember ever having heard that sound before. Was it the wind? Outside the trees were still, but the sound seemed to be rushing in about them like a tornado.

Simon and several other men jumped to their feet. Someone opened a window shutter wide, looking for danger. As Mary watched in fear, a ball of flames appeared out of nowhere over their heads and began to break and shower down on the group. A flame appeared over Peter, and then over Matthew—and Andrew—and all the Twelve she could see. Frightened, she looked about for Mary Magdalene. Mary always knew what to do in a strange situation. But Mary was all the way across the room, and as she watched a fire appeared over her head, too! Scanning those near her, Mary could see the flames lapping gently over the heads of each person. Instinctively she reached above her own veil. Simon caught her eye from a few feet away, smiled, and nodded in amazement. She reached out to him, thankful that he was there.

"It's The Power," Simon said quietly. "The Power has fallen. The Promise is fulfilled."

All over the room truth was dawning like the sunshine. "It's the Spirit!" "We are receiving Power!" First in whispers, and then in joyful shouts, "The Spirit has come—the Promise is true!" "Praise Jesus, he has sent his Power!" Friends were moving about the room, hugging and crying and praying as the reality of the Gift grew. Some dropped to their knees; others threw their arms open wide to receive all they could hold. The Day of Pentecost was being fulfilled before their eyes, and Mary marveled in jubilation and praise.

Closing her eyes and cupping her hands over her face in prayer, Mary spoke aloud. "You are back, my son, my Lord," she said softly. "You have come back to us on wings of power. I feel you in my deepest soul, inside the holy place of my heart. Oh, Jesus! You have sent your Spirit. You are here!"

Outside a crowd was gathering below. Someone was knocking at the upstairs door; others were ringing the bell at the front gate, shouting: "What's going on in there?" "What is all this noise? Come out and tell us what's going on!" "Are you drunk? Have you lost your minds?" *The wind noise must be real,* Mary thought, *and others outside our group are hearing it, too.*

Believers began spilling out of the room and down both stairways, into the street, everyone talking at once. "It's Jesus! It's Jesus!" they assured their neighbors joyfully. "He has sent us his Spirit! He is alive—God has raised him back to life—and today he has sent us his Power!"

Mary found John on the outer steps about halfway down, watching the believers as they mixed among holiday pilgrims on their way to morning prayers at the temple. "Pentecost will never be the same," she said quietly.

John hugged her close and smiled. "Neither will we, Aunt Mary. Neither will we."

Changes in the Church: Acts 2:37–47

Talk about a growing, changing church! How did those one hundred twenty original believers ever assimilate three thousand new people into their fellowship? Who could learn so many names? Where did they find enough water to baptize that many converts? Where did they get enough bread for the Lord's Supper on a regular basis? How did they all fit into any place of worship? What happened to the intimacy they had clung to so desperately in the Upper Room all those weeks? Mary was in the middle of all that, too. Knowing how hard change comes, we have to stand in awe of the spirit of that group in those days of overflowing blessings. We might have been standing in the street saying, "Stop, Lord! Stop! It is too much!"

Of course it was the Holy Spirit who effected the changes, and then gave grace to the believers that allowed them to cope, and seize the opportunity for greater spiritual power. Is he best called the "Holy Spirit," the "Spirit of God," or, the "Spirit of Jesus?" Actually, Scripture refers to him in all three ways and more. Luke, in this story, calls him "the Holy Spirit" (Acts 2:4). Jesus promised him as "the Holy Spirit whom the Father will send in my name," and says, "I will not leave you as orphans; I will come to you." (Find his teaching on this in John 14:15–18, 25–26 and surrounding verses.) Paul refers to him as "the Spirit of Jesus Christ" in Philippians 1:19. Again we confront the mystery of the Trinity, the Three Manifestations of God, and we see once more how inadequate we are to sort it out fully.

Well, to be truthful about the changing church, problems did arise—a little later. But the good news is: the church didn't self-destruct. It continued to grow to five thousand and more in those first months. Eventually, through the obedience of the Apostles and later Paul and his associates, the message spread, until it blanketed the entire Roman Empire and even beyond.

It was Jesus' church, empowered by his Spirit, guided by his plan. But never forget, at the start of it all was one brave, young Jewish girl who answered, "I am the Lord's servant. May it be to me as you have said…My soul praises the Lord and my spirit rejoices in God, my Savior, for he has been mindful of the humble estate of his servant. From now on all generations will call me blessed."

To order additional copies of

A *Touch* of *Jesus*

Have your credit card ready and call:

1-877-421-READ (7323)

or please visit our web site at
www.pleasantword.com

Also available at:
www.amazon.com
and
www.barnesandnoble.com

Printed in the United States
119520LV00001B/1-96/A